SHONALI SABHERWAL

THE BEAUTY DIET
EAT YOUR WAY TO A FAB NEW YOU

RANDOM HOUSE INDIA

Published by Random House India in 2012
Fourth impression in 2012

Random House Publishers India Private Limited
Windsor IT Park, 7th Floor, Tower-B,
A-1, Sector-125, Noida-201301 (UP)

Random House Group Limited
20 Vauxhall Bridge Road
London SW1V 2SA
United Kingdom

ISBN 978 81 8400 196 9

Typeset in Sabon by InoSoft Systems, Noida

Printed and bound in India by Replika Press Private Limited

To my dad,
who brought me to macrobiotics.
And Brian,
without whom it would not have been possible.
To you, readers—
hope you find the secrets helpful.
And to the Divine,
for whom I am a mere channel of this wisdom.

CONTENTS

Part Two

Part Three

FOREWORD

Just as exercise is important for a well-toned body, food is vital for overall beauty, which includes a slim body with glowing skin and healthy hair. When you eat well, you nourish the body and your blood circulation and digestion get stimulated. This immediately creates an overall vitality and that unmistakable secret glow. In today's life, it's important not only to look a certain way, but to also feel confident about yourself. And that only comes from feeling healthy and beautiful. And who doesn't want beauty as one of their virtues, right? I too wanted to look and feel like a million dollars. And that's where the challenge lay.

It is extremely difficult to find genuine health-food products and places to find them. When I first came to Mumbai, I struggled to find food products that were healthy and nutritious, and which also kept my hunger pangs at bay since most of what is out there in the market is artificial and processed. I was looking for something different. That's when I read about Shonali in the papers.

Shonali believes in an organic, a well-balanced and simple diet, and her outlook towards food matched mine. I called her immediately. This was two years ago, during the promotions of my film *Alladin*. I have been with her for over two years now.

When I started eating with Shonali I was worried that her diet included too much carbs. I had avoided rice, bread, and beans ever since I started watching my weight, but I soon put my fears to bed as the benefits of Shonali's approach were immediately visible. The first change that was evident to me as well as to the people around me was that my skin and hair both started looking healthy and vibrant. Before I met Shonali, I suffered from PCOS (polycystic ovarian syndrome) and constant stomach problems, and my weight fluctuated because of the various diets I was on. But after Shonali's food, those issues never returned. It was then that I realized that in my quest to look good and be thin, I had actually invited many other problems by eating less. But that is all in the past now.

After being introduced to her approach, I started looking better than I ever had. I was happier and healthier, and I could do more intensive workouts because I had more energy. I was actually feeling like a kid again, like I was eating mum's food. I always joke that Shonali is my 'tiffin mum'. However, the best thing about her food is that you don't end up craving unhealthy food; she balances the meals and gives you the right amount of complex carbs so I always feel satisfied and full, and don't feel like I need cheat meals because there's always variety in Shonali's food. Through Shonali's food, I've discovered a whole new side of me. Apart from my skin never breaking out and my hair looking thick and glossy, I've actually been able to maintain my weight. By the time I was shooting *Murder 2* I was toned and fit naturally. That's what following Shonali's approach has done for me.

The Beauty Diet can open up doors to beauty that you never thought existed. And the funny thing is that that there's actually nothing to it. Here, the emphasis is on understanding the importance of a well-balanced meal. All natural foods are good for you, even carbs like sweet potatoes. A healthy mixture of carbs, protein, and good fats should constitute each meal, and that is the basis of looking and feeling great. Staying away from processed and refined food keeps your body detoxified and functioning properly. And that's where Shonali steps in. She not only explains the importance of food, but also the kind of food that will benefit you the most. *The Beauty Diet* is packed with secrets of everyday foods, things that we see but never pay any attention to. This is the most comprehensive guide to lead you to a healthier and more beautiful you, and my secret which I want to share with all my fans and readers of this book.

A final word. Forget diets which are temporary—the real test is having something that works for you in the long term and being able to maintain that so that it's ingrained in your daily life. When it comes to looking your best, give your body the best tools to help it achieve that. Never sell yourself short; good food is like a lifetime investment with high returns. The power to be healthy and beautiful lies in your hands and yours completely. So what are you waiting for—let's all embrace good health and get beautiful.

Jacqueline Fernandez
Mumbai

INTRODUCTION

Take a look at the image of Goddess Kali. Dishevelled hair, raging eyes, she is poised on Shiva, wearing a garland of human heads, and a skirt of human limbs. But have you ever noticed how she's biting on her tongue? My friend Rohit Arya, who writes on mythology and spirituality, revealed to me what the biting of the tongue symbolizes. The tongue is the prime symbol of passions as it is the centre for taste, regarded as the core passion. Once you can control your craving, not only for food, but also for rasa—flavour or taste in all its connotations—you have won over your passions. Kali biting her tongue is an acknowledgement of her control over the passions of the world. Literally, she has conquered the palate, the desire for flavour, for taste or for rasa, one of the hardest things to do in yoga. But sadly that is not what we humans do; most people I meet would like to get the juice out of life when it comes to food.

By this I don't mean you should turn into yogis or eat nuts and leaves and live out in the wilderness. The idea is to control our urges and live a balanced life. Balance is vital. It is what keeps the body and mind fit, healthy, and harmonized. Through this book I will explain how balance is the secret to good health and beauty.

Beauty is really skin deep, and that's why food and true beauty are linked very closely together. We all love being beautiful. But is beauty just having good, proportionate physical attributes? Or is it that glow that shouts over your physical attributes, the vitality, as I call it, of your being? If it is our prerogative to be beautiful, then it becomes necessary to be healthy. That 'glow' and 'vitality' are a result of good health, not cosmetics and products to make you look beautiful superficially. It is food upon which the whole structure of your beauty rests. Your skin, hair, and nails are all the result of what food choices you make and how your organs work to process this food. Eat healthy—well at least 80 percent of the time—and you will be awarded with true beauty.

The only factors that are important in achieving true beauty is a diet of good, wholesome, and natural everyday food, a balanced approach to eating, a regular lifestyle, exercise, and daily care of your body. As each chapter in this book unfolds the mystery of how food really works for you, you will realize that what you eat has a direct impact on how you look and your vitality.

How did I get into all of this?

My brush with getting myself healthy began when my dad was diagnosed with prostate cancer in 1998. The cancer had progressed beyond the gland and spread to his bones, and there was very little the doctors could do. They gave us a life expectancy of three years with radiation and pain medication as a prognosis. We were crushed, but life has a strange way of working out. His cancer came with a gift—a gift that changed my life completely. I am the first-born in a family of three children, and closest to my father. He often called me his 'twin soul', and when tragedy struck, he looked to me for support in every way. I had three years to save him.

Cancer is hard, both on the patient and the family. I remember living from one Prostate-Specific Antigen test to the other. (PSA tests detect the levels of protein in blood produced by the prostate gland. Increased levels are an indication that the cancer has spread beyond the gland. The higher the PSA level, the more cancer cells present in the body.) My father's PSA levels were completely out of control. One day a friend's mother told us about an approach called macrobiotics which is said to be able to reverse cancer. Here began my search for an alternative way of living for my father. Our search led us to an American lady, Mona Schwartz, in Dehradun who was an old proponent of this approach. Mona taught my mother and me the basics of the foods used in macrobiotics. We trained in her kitchen and learnt about the approach. However, it was the reading that I did in Mona's library over the ten days of our stay there, which was revealing. I was already a Vipassana meditator and understood the effects of energy in our bodies, but did not know that food and cooking styles also had energy components, and that their correct combinations could produce subtle energy changes within the body. That was it for me. I knew then that I wanted to learn more about this approach, and that I had found my true calling.

Back in Mumbai, my mother and I started applying the approach to my father's life. But we were still amateurs.

It is important to make interesting and exciting food for a person who is undergoing radiation and is on a lot of medication. Unfortunately, since I was not trained at that time the way I am today, I could do only so much with my limited knowledge. My father was a true north Indian when it came to his food and palette, and he soon gave up on our food and went back to his old eating habits. He passed away in 2001.

In 2005, I started researching how I could pursue macrobiotics further. By then I was also diagnosed with a slipped disc. Little did I know that my body was in complete rebellion with years of erratic eating habits. I decided to pursue two courses—first, a Counsellor and Chef's certification at the Kushi Institute in Massachusetts, and second, a Yoga Pilates course in Australia. Here began a journey that changed the definition of health for me and the course of my life.

Once I was trained as a chef and a health counsellor, I knew I had to combine both roles to make something happen. I also knew that it would take some time to convince people about how serious health conditions could be reversed using this approach. I cook with passion, working at it like a director who carefully crafts his scenes or a writer piecing together his story. I knew the first thing I had to do was to get my food out to people. So I went to the market, got myself a new fridge and cooking gear, and the basics to start with. I started with five clients and no advertising or publicity. But the food I was dishing out soon started to speak for itself, and that's when everything began falling into place.

Steve Gagné, author of the book *Food Energetics*, says, 'When you choose, eat, digest, assimilate and absorb, utilize, and animate the cells of your food, a process far more vital than "burning fuel" takes place. Indeed, in every sense you merge with those foods. They become you and you become them, too. In the merging what emerges? Not simply a well-fuelled machine, but a slightly new you. It is not "consumption" but a living union—"consummation" that might be the more apt term! In choosing your foods, you not only choose to "be nourished", you choose specific qualities in your foods that nourish those qualities in yourself.'

What Gagné means is that we must shift our focus from consumption to nourishment to make changes in our bodies. And *The Beauty Diet* aims to do just that. Through this book, I'll teach you how to understand food and its energies, foods that will work for you, and foods that will help to mitigate the negative effects of other foods. I will help you learn the art of balancing your tastes, and use food to cleanse your system. Beauty lies in nature and we can heal ourselves and be beautiful with simple everyday foods. Put your faith in nature, and it will reward you. Like the great Romantic poet William Wordsworth once said, 'Come forth into the light of things, let nature be your teacher.'

WHAT IS MACROBIOTICS?

Macrobiotics, or the big view of life (in Greek, macro means great and bios means life), was first used in literature by a German physicist, Christoph Wilhelm Hufeland. His book *Macrobiotics: The Art of Prolonging Human Life* explores macrobiotics as a science aimed at prolonging and perfecting life. According to Hufeland, macrobiotics is a medical philosophy on a higher level than the curative, preventative, or health levels of medicine.

George Ohsawa, the founder of macrobiotics, formulated his own philosophy on diet and health by familiarizing himself with Hufeland's work. Ohsawa himself recovered from tuberculosis of the lungs after using healing foods recommended by a military doctor. He came up with his own philosophy on macrobiotics and travelled the world spreading his ideas. One of Ohsawa's students, Michio Kushi, decided to propagate this approach in America in the 1960s. He first started with being a natural-foods distributor and then established the Kushi Institute in 1978, where I studied this approach to health.

The healing powers of the foods used in macrobiotics came into focus when Dr Anthony J. Sattilaro published his book *Recalled by Life*, wherein he traced his journey of recovery from prostate cancer. This was when macrobiotics first gained popularity as a cancer-curing approach. And then the approach gained momentum as the secret behind these healing foods was revealed by people who adopted them into their lives.

Macrobiotics is neither folk medicine, nor a mystical, palliative, religious, scientific, spiritual, or symptomatic technique. It is the biological and physiological application of Oriental philosophy and medicine, and an understanding of the energies of food. Very simply, it focuses on choosing the right foods and cooking styles and putting them into practice.

The macrobiotic approach is ideally suited for the Indian environment as well as intrinsically in tune with its ethos because a macrobiotic diet is, by unconscious design, as close to a perfect sattvic diet as you could hope for. The approach focuses on cleaning out the nadis or meridians in the body for optimum functioning.

Culturally and historically India is naturally receptive to the macrobiotic ideal. Our cuisine is predominantly one of whole grains and vegetables. In fact, we as Indians do not have to make major shifts in attitude to adopt a macrobiotic diet; it only requires some minor readjustments. Anyone can adopt it in their daily life, anywhere, anytime, if they genuinely want to be free of all physiological and mental strains.

How to Read This Book

My goal with this book is to give you simple secrets to using everyday foods to attain a healthy and beautiful you. Since the content of this book stems out of an approach grounded in a rich history of healthy eating, building strong immunity, and giving you true beauty from everyday simple foods, it is best to begin with the basics and start reading it from the start.

Part I lays down the foundation of 'what works' and 'what does not work' with respect to our changed lifestyle habits. As a trained macrobiotic counsellor and chef, I use a lot of diagnostic tools with my clients to find out what state of health they are in when they come to me. I also use these tools to find out how the organs are working as it is closely connected to how we look. I have tried to explain all this in Part I in a simple and accessible way. Here I will debunk the many myths associated with dairy. Part I also teaches you the basic ground rules of being healthy and beautiful, how your organs work to help you digest and assimilate the food you eat every day, the basic approach to your beauty diet, nutritional value of special foods as well as food combinations that will work for you, and how these foods affect your emotional quotient. The icing on the cake is when I bring in my added expertise as a chef, and take you through the kitchen FAQs. I have freely used case histories of celebrities and clients that I have worked with to show you how I went about helping them achieve their goals.

Part II lays out the actual plan to achieve a beautiful you. Here, I share with you diets that help you apply the basics of health and beauty talked about in Part I. The section begins with what is a detox, how to do it, and a 3- and 7-day detox diet, what foods work for your face and skin, hair, vitality, and also slow down the ageing process. The USP of this section, I feel, is basic 7-day diet plans separately for each beauty element: so we have a face, skin, and hair diet, a healthy weight diet for a fab body, and an anti-ageing diet. I follow a lot of simple home remedies to achieve certain objectives like controlling your sugar cravings or getting rid of those fat cells. There is also a workbook to get you started and show you where you are: so after Part II you have done your own mini diagnosis with the tools provided in Part I and also know where and why your problem is occurring, now you need part III to implement the Beauty Diet.

Part III is the execution section where I have actually given you useful recipes, some of which I have used in the diet plans and reiterated throughout the book. For me this is the most practical section of the book, which makes the book user-friendly and leaves no doubt as to what to eat, how to use a recipe, and so on. I feel only diets are not enough, but with actual recipes you are more likely to achieve your beauty goals at the earliest. Not only that, these are easy to make recipes that you can incorporate in your daily diet, and make it part of your lifestyle.

I have tried to make the book interesting for you by adding charts and tables which make it an interesting read. Throughout the book there are quick tips, descriptions on extra supplements you may need, and beauty formulas that will work for you. I also relate everything I say back to my own life, and how I have dealt with my own health issues—what has helped me get here being the healthiest I have ever been, with a perfect body weight, and looking years younger that I actually am.

Tempting? Then go ahead and read the book to a new and fab you! I will make every page count in this transformation to a new you.

PART ONE

1

FOOD AND BEAUTY

Beauty is priceless

Sunday, and you were being a mall rat. The luxurious new body products line, which boasts of everything from Dead Sea bathing salts to yummy dark chocolate scrubs and rich caviar cream, drew you in like a moth to a flame. You loaded up your basket with a heap of these goodies, each promising to make you look younger and giving you that 'glow' to die for, and leaving you feeling good about yourself, albeit with a lighter wallet.

Well who can blame you? You gave into luscious advertising and the promise of a quick fix. But do you really think you can look younger and be more beautiful by using an inch-high bottle of caviar cream worth Rs 5000? Wouldn't we all look fabulous all the time if we just knew which magic potion worked for us? I'm sorry to bring it down so hard, but that little tub of cream does nothing but moisturize your skin and cause a dent in your bank balance. Beauty doesn't come in a container or a tube. It cannot be bought. Period.

Everyone has an idea of their 'best self'—one with spotless, glowing skin, a head full of shiny, healthy hair, a lean body, clear eyes, pearly white teeth, and nails that never ever break without good reason. You want to be beautiful. You want to look like a vision, like your favourite Hollywood star, all the time. Today, more than ever, people are ultra-conscious about the way they look. First impressions count, and you want yours to be fabulous. Pick up any glossy magazine and you're bound to get tips on '10 ways to get youthful-looking skin' or '5 shortcuts to a leaner body'. There is huge pressure on you to look your best, to be fit, and most importantly, to look young. But how do you achieve that if you've also got a million other tasks to complete in a mere 24 hours? You're working round the clock to keep up with the rat race and so your health and lifestyle take a backseat. But you still want to look gorgeous.

Here's the thing. You can do all those million things and still look fabulous while you're doing them. To get to a beautiful you, there's just one path that needs to be taken. One that doesn't involve spending a huge chunk of your money on expensive lotions, potions, shampoos, and creams. And that is food. I kid you not. Beauty lies in what we eat and not on what we slather on our skins. Just as polluted fuel will ruin the engine of a car, bad food habits cause nothing but harm to our bodies. The old adage is true—beauty really does start from within. And it has everything to do with what you eat.

You are what you eat

The philosophy behind looking great is actually quite basic. There is no stronger argument for natural beauty than the old saying 'you are what you eat'. Starting a nutrient-rich, health- and beauty-food diet calls for just a few basic, yet healthy changes in the way you currently eat. Food affects all the cells in our body, and by extension, every aspect of our being—mood, energy levels, food cravings, thinking capacity, sex drive, and sleep patterns. If you feed your body junk and convenience foods, it'll definitely show; and trust me, no fancy caviar creams can hide the damage. The bottom line is that being beautiful is much more than just a diet. **It's a lifestyle.**

Now you must be thinking, 'I barely have time to brush my teeth in the morning, how on earth do I fix myself an all-nutritious breakfast? The task seems Herculean and unnecessary, especially when there's that cafe bang next to office serving up those scrumptious crêpes. And there's always that miraculous diet that'll help me lose five kilos in a week. So who needs breakfast?'

Wrong, wrong, and wrong once again. Binge eating and then resorting to crash diets, unnatural remedies, and a reliance on diet myths will cause irreversible damage to your system. Eating right may seem difficult in the beginning, especially if you've been an erratic eater for years. But take it from me, there is no other alternative to it. Everything else is temporary and cheating!

Here's where I step in. I speak from experience. Before macrobiotics, I was edgy, hated my thighs, and had an incessant candida problem. But once I got into it, the macrobiotics lifestyle changed my life. After practising it strictly for six years, and about 70 percent of it for four years before that, I have reached a stage where I have not taken any medication in ten years, have immense amounts of energy, and maintain a regular weight. I also often get asked what foundation I use (when I actually use none) and have hair that my stylist loves to cut as there is just so much of it. I am super driven and focussed and am constantly reinventing myself. I couldn't have asked for anything more. It's called 'the beauty diet' for a reason, and it deals with the basic issue of understanding food vis a vis your body's needs.

As a health practitioner, I know that there are many misconceptions floating around about what is construed as healthy. We are seeing lifestyle diseases grow and health conditions worsen, forcing us to take stock of our health and lives. In a paper written on 'Lifestyle Diseases from an Indian Perspective', Jhilam Rudra Re, a lecturer at the NSHM College of Management and Technology Kolkata, cites that the World Health Organization (WHO) in a recent study has declared India a nation that will have the most lifestyle diseases in the near future. For example, India leads in the number of cardiac patients at 10 percent of the population compared to other countries like US/UK at 7 percent and China at 4 percent. Fifty million people suffer from heart problems and this figure doubled in 2010; with the highest growth rate amongst young executives— one in eight of these people being under the age of forty. India is called the diabetic capital of the world with as many as thirty million patients, and this number is growing by the day. But, because Indians are on the brink of something amazing when it comes to re-claiming their health, it makes my work as a practitioner and chef more exciting.

Education is the key here and it is vital to know that what works for one person may not necessarily work for another. For example, if I have a thyroid condition and you have hypoglycemia, although the basic structure of our diets may remain the same, we still need to know what foods will work better in healing our condition. The macrobiotic diet busts a lot of myths about food and lays bare the essentials of a healthy and balanced diet that does nothing but wonders for your body. The diet sounds complicated but it is not. The crux of it lies in finding the right food for you (I call it soul food). And once you get on to it, I can guarantee you'll be hooked. Just ask Katrina Kaif. ☺

KATRINA KAIF AND THE BEAUTY DIET

'I can't believe a bowl of brown rice porridge will not make me gain weight!' Katrina balked at my suggestion of the aforementioned gruel.

I told her firmly, 'I am not an actress, you are; but I know my onions when it comes to food. So you stick to all the good acting you have planned, while I will stick to all the healthy food I cook. And if you gain weight, we'll stop.'

But we didn't stop.

Katrina discovered me quite by chance. The owner of a specialty food store that had opened near her place knew that I catered healthy food from my kitchen for various clients on a daily basis. So she asked

Katrina to contact me, as she was looking for someone to cook her wholesome but interesting meals daily, and counsel her on her diet.

I met her on a shoot later in the week. It was a rushed meeting, but she established two factors pretty quickly:

1. She wanted to keep her energy levels high as her work demanded it.
2. She wanted to keep her weight stable.

Katrina also mentioned that she wanted to stay off carbohydrates completely (which I did not agree with at that point, but I decided that I would convince her otherwise later), and that she wanted to incorporate fish in her evening meals. With that we got started. I taught Saeeda, her personal assistant, where to source ingredients from, how to stock a pantry, etc.

Making the meals interesting is always the least of my worries because that's where my expertise as a chef comes in. But to fulfil the objectives that a client seeks while ensuring that the food provides benefits beyond what one can physically see is the crucial part. Much as she didn't want it, I knew that I wasn't going to cut out complex carbohydrates from her diet, as they are the foundation of a body. And after some amount of convincing, I got her to agree to that bowl of brown rice porridge (see recipe on p 257) in the mornings.

Katrina's meals included complex carbs in the form of brown rice or rotis. Her lunch was centred on a larger component of vegetables (65 percent) rather than beans/fish (35 percent) and her dinners always included a hearty soup with miso (see Recipe section for soups) thrown in to activate the digestive enzymes and vegetables. The thing that Katrina loved about my food was the variety in the cuisines that I brought into play here to keep things interesting. We did everything from Moroccan, Greek, Italian, Mexican, Indian,

Caribbean, and Thai to Japanese, and a whole lot more. It kept her curious and asking for more. Whoever said a diet is dull and boring has obviously not eaten my food. ☺

The food I was giving her was free of sugar, dairy, processed white flour, yeast, and gluten, and provided her with sustained levels of blood sugar. The use of the right oils (liquid fat) was also critical to keep her weight under check. It was keeping her energy levels high, which was top priority for me. I applied my secrets (which I will soon share with you) of various cooking styles in her meals, so she was always energetic. I especially used styles which spread the energy of food outward and upward (sautéing, boiling, and blanching) in the day, and then styles like baking or grilling her fish, and pressure cooking in the evenings, which would shift the energy inward, because then I wanted her energy to settle.

One such cooking style is the nishime (see recipe on p 263) which I used a lot. Nishime literally means 'waterless cooking'; the vegetables cook in their own juices. It also stabilizes blood sugar levels, releases pressure, and gives slow sustained energy. In my training, cooking styles are also used to impart energy and just not the food. The nishime cooking style works like a steam engine in your system, giving you the energy that a turbine pump uses to generate electricity! This is mainly because of the way the vegetables cook in this style: cook in a heavy cast iron pot (usually a creuset), add minimal water, and don't touch the dish for a good twenty minutes. The energy that is generated within the pot is that of the vegetables releasing water and cooking in their own juices on a slow fire. The energy is upward and inward and circulates in that fashion. So when I look at the yin and yang of cooking, this style has both elements in perfect balance, as within the pot it's like a steam engine (internal generator) for twenty minutes, giving the same energy to anyone who uses it. I highly recommend the nishime style to cancer patients suffering from low energy and people who need a boost of energy. I used it for Katrina as she needed this energy to sustain her throughout her day. It's very easy, so have a look at the end of the book in the Recipe section.

I also used vegetables very cleverly. Since she did not want too many complex carbohydrates in a grain format for lunch or dinner, I included more vegetables (50–60 percent) instead of whole grains. I used a lot of upward growing, leafy greens and green onions, carrots and white radish (it's a little known secret that white radish is great for dissolving fats for fibre; all of which would give her a much lighter yin effect (explained in Chapter 2). In the evenings, I used more round vegetables like turnips, squash, and beets, which added an inward yang effect (explained in Chapter 2), to settle her energy yet give her a boost when combined with stronger cooking styles like nishime, slow boiling, stewing, and grilling.

Change is not always visible at first, but when change does occur it does not go unnoticed. Katrina was very appreciative and wholeheartedly spoke to the press about the food she was eating and its benefits—a sign that it was all working. 'It's amazing how much variety there is in the food, and how the food gives me so much energy. I feel great,' Katrina said about this approach.

A good diet doesn't show results overnight. It's not supposed to. If you're on a random diet, losing weight by the hour, it's time to get off that bus. When my clients come in for a session, I teach them how to 'layer' their diet week by week. Take one component of the programme and build on it every week. We are not entering a beauty pageant here; the goal is to not only lose weight, but to also gain health, change our blood condition—as it takes the body ten days to replace all its white blood cells, so eating foods which have a strong living energy will influence your blood condition. In four months the body changes all its red blood cells; so eating a healthy diet for such a duration will impact your blood condition and all the outward manifestations in skin, hair, age, and vitality and get you that 'to-die-for' glow.

Your face—the mirror to your body

Your face reveals much more about your insides than you know. Hidden behind your facial elements is the history of your body, blood condition, and what ails it. I spend a lot of time with each of my clients and since I only do one consultation a day, I give the person on the other end enough time. My diagnosis starts the moment a client walks in. I can look at your toes and bunions and tell if your diet was rich in saturated fat as a child, and whether you eat a lot of chicken and meat. How do I know? Simple. The body cannot process certain types of foods, and they have a way of accumulating in particular areas of the body (your bunions are a result of too much saturated fat and chicken). Sounds unbelievable, but it's true. Pimples are your body's way of eliminating foods consumed in excess. If they are around your eyelids, they indicate an elimination of protein, fat, and sugar, caused by the overconsumption of fruit and meats. Even the way your mother ate when she was pregnant with you can be easily determined. Eyelids that are swollen, red, or purple indicate excessive intake of fruits, sugar and other sweets, soda, soft drinks, alcohol, and other stimulants. And this is just the warm up to the diagnosis. It's all written large on your face. But more on that in Part II (see p 187).

When painter Lili Menon came to me, she had already given up on other 'diets'. She told me that she felt bloated and experienced discomfort because of it, and that her movements were restricted. She felt like she was trapped in an old body that was slowing her down. What she didn't know then was that her system was beginning to get sluggish.

Her large intestine meridian indicated some discomfort on touch, her tongue was coated; the tongue should normally be pink. A coated tongue is a sign of candida (bad bacteria/yeast in the body that has built up over time due to the consumption of foods which do not assimilate properly and putrefy). Candida can cause many problems, and in Lili's case it manifested as a bloated body, a puffy face, and fatigue. I knew exactly how to fix her situation. What surprised Lili was that the diagnosis was bang on target, and the approach was tailor made for her.

To reverse her growth of candida, I needed to do two things:

1) Restore the inner environment of the body, thus preventing the growth of more candida.
2) Maintain and develop the internal environment of the digestive system to sustain the new friendly and good bacteria which needed to be introduced to bring back the natural balance.

It was a two-pronged attack to restore immunity and balance.

So while the base of Lili's diet remained whole grains, beans, vegetables, and some fish, I took her off the stuff that feeds the yeast, such as breads, wines, alcohol, sugar, antibiotics, and dairy, which help bad bacteria thrive by keeping the system damp from inside. I also introduced fermented foods (which helped to reintroduce good bacteria) such as miso in her soup (see benefits in chapter 5 under the Fermented Foods section), brown rice idlis (by fermenting them with the miso), quick pickles, and pressed salads (see Vegetable section for recipe).

This is what Lili had to say after following the Beauty Diet:

'What this approach did for me was that it gave me my body and health back. For me to be 'normal' and feel fit was a great feeling. This approach moved me from a diet to a lifestyle and gave me the freedom to eat and live well. It's only when you go through it yourself that you realize the difference between a diet and a lifestyle change. I don't want to stop ever. Maybe I will allow myself certain leeways, but will never veer to the big NOs.

The good thing about this approach is that it has been adapted to the Indian climate and palate as well. **It's a total lifestyle change.** And it is easy to stick to, even in the Indian context or internationally. Once you understand it, you work it out. Even if you don't, you learn to balance yourself out.'

Eating with freedom

Any approach to eating, since that is what we humans do on a 24 hour-basis, should come with an element of freedom—the freedom to live with great health and a trouble-free mind, and freedom from limitations that a diet would impose. You should know that every single morsel you put in your mouth has a direct impact on this freedom.

The more natural foods you eat, the more freely your inner self flows.

Jessica Porter, macrobiotic chef and author of the popular book *The Hip Chick's Guide to Macrobiotics,* says the trick is to discover your own inner compass and then follow its direction; once you do that, all limitations become obsolete. Each person's requirements and objectives are different. My body will respond differently from yours, as we have different constitutions and conditions. Freedom also comes with the fact that you are free to make your own choices when reading this book, applying the suggestions and seeing the consequences.

When I first started this approach, I was very rigid and would feel bad when I vacillated between the new approach and my old habits. I wanted to achieve a healthy state of being, quickly. But I gradually came to realize that until you practise, apply, and learn from your mistakes, it's no fun. I did just that—I started cooking for myself, slipped, got up, reapplied what I had learnt and then learnt a whole lot more out of the experience. On a spiritual canvas, I feel an inner sense of calm and a connection to things around me. Negativity is not a feeling I possess in my life any more. I can safely say that I do not have any negative relationships; I am full of compassion and gratitude. To me that is a sign of wellness and beauty.

What we're going to work on

This book has three main points on which the diet is based. These three factors are the foundation of your change. And they don't involve earth-shattering changes. In the following chapters, we'll be focussing on these three important factors:

1) Understanding the basic make-up of food and its energies
2) Why and what we should and shouldn't eat
3) How food can change us

If you get these principles right, you're already well on your way to the path of being healthy.

The gradual change

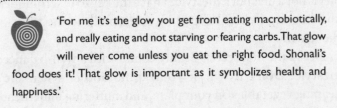

'For me it's the glow you get from eating macrobiotically, and really eating and not starving or fearing carbs. That glow will never come unless you eat the right food. Shonali's food does it! That glow is important as it symbolizes health and happiness.'

JACQUELINE FERNANDEZ—ACTOR

Now comes the tough bit. The mind is where the change must happen first. But it always resists change vehemently, though it also gets accustomed to things or a way of life very easily. That's why we develop habits. Once you start trying to get healthy, your desire for junk food may go up, as your mind will start resisting the wholesome foods you are giving your body. But have patience. Rome wasn't built in a day.

It takes time for the effect of these foods to kick in, and for the right nutrients to start working to help decrease your cravings. Our bodies change much slower than the rate at which our thought processes change. Allow yourself the slips—acknowledge them and move on. Don't be too hard on yourself, as that is a negative reaction to what you are doing. Breathe. That cheese and pepperoni pizza you had for lunch today won't kill you. It's okay. If you try too hard or restrict yourself too much, your body's insulin levels may be thrown off balance. Don't be rigid; the moment you are aware of your urges, you'll have a better chance at controlling them and avoid making a slip. I repeat, like a sergeant in a drill: remember a well-balanced diet is not a diet but a **lifestyle**. That's the key to macrobiotics, and healthy living. Keep it up and you'll be the toast of the town.

Here's the first secret. Beauty comes with a well-balanced lifestyle. Don't frown at your grandmother when she's heaping vegetables on your plate, and muttering underneath her breath, 'you are what you eat'. She's right. So, if you're ready to transform your relationship with food and achieve a higher level of wellness, let's get started.

2

THE ENERGY OF FOOD

Why and what do we eat?

It's 1.30 pm and you have fifteen minutes to grab something before you get back to your desk and to that presentation you were working on. Your stomach is growling so you know you have to eat...something, anything. But fifteen minutes isn't time for a leisurely lunch, so you opt for that sandwich instead. There, lunch and hunger both taken care of. How many of us have done that or are grabbing that sandwich as I speak? Admit it. We've all been guilty of it. This brings to light an interesting question—why do we eat? Do we eat only because we are hungry, or do we eat for other reasons?

Most people eat because we know it's time to eat, or eat because it satisfies a basic primal instinct, that of hunger. Hunger is the physiological need for food. It's something that we just must satisfy. But this 'eating to survive' makes eating routine and boring. You don't think twice about it or are not conscious about what you are putting into your mouth. You just well...eat.

But food is more than just survival. Food nourishes our bodies and supplies us with energy and is necessary for carrying out basic physiological processes that keep us alive. We need this energy to carry out activities for daily living. Food is vital. So much so that the **right food has the ability to change your blood condition in four months,** as I mentioned earlier (in four months all your red blood cells change with good living food!), **and your entire cell structure in just two years!** It also provides us with the right neurotransmitters, such as serotonin, which leads to a balanced and calm mind. So here is the next secret. You can actually create a completely new you by eating right.

We all go through life with some major or minor forms of ill health, ranging from a common cold or cough to allergies, backaches, premenstrual cramping, etc. It is only after a major illness hits us or a family member that we get up and take notice of what we might be doing wrong in our lives. But how many of us actually blame our diets? This largely stems from the fact that on an average people are ignorant and unaware of what constitutes 'good health'.

When the body throws you a symptom, be it minor or major, it's actually the body's way of saying, 'Look at me. There's something going on here. You've done something to cause this.' However, once we go to the doc and he or she diagnoses us, we're content with popping those antibiotics and other drugs. Here's the thing. These minor ailments are bound to resurface—if not in three, four, five months, then a year, because all we did was use a quick-fix solution. And we'll find ourselves back at the doc's clinic, where he'll be signing us away with a new prescription of newer drugs. This, my dear, is the vicious circle that most of us are trapped in.

If you are reading this book, there is something that has motivated you to get healthier, and when you're healthy, you automatically become beautiful. One of the tenets of eating right is that if we come from this earth, then it has the power to heal us as well. The goal with food is to feel vitalized by it, not be depleted by depriving ourselves of it. Food has its triggers also, so if you ingest the wrong foods, the triggers created by these foods will lead you to eat more wrong foods, which will make you ill, put on weight, have bad skin or skin disorders, and lose hair. And these you want to avoid, don't you? But first, let's understand the basic make-up of foods after which I will tell you the 5 mantras for a beautiful you.

The fine balance

Eastern philosophy believes that every living thing has energy, be it you, your pet, vegetables (see chart on Yin and Yang foods p 21), even a stone. And these energies are the life force which, when balanced, result in harmony of the negative and positive. The law is so simple that it becomes profound in a larger context.

Look at any naturally occurring phenomenon and you'll find it. Sun and moon; night and day; water and fire; winter and summer. The clever ancient Chinese philosophers simplified this into the symbol of **yin** and **yang**.

THE TWO LIFE FORCES: YIN AND YANG

The outer circle represents 'everything', while the black and white shapes within the circle represent the two energies—yin (black) and yang (white). However, they are not completely black or white, just as things in life are never black or white, and they cannot exist without each other.

Yin is dark, passive, downward, cold, contracting, and weak.

Yang is bright, active, upward, hot, expanding, and strong.

The shape of the yin and yang sections of the symbol actually gives you a sense of the continual movement of these two energies, yin to yang and yang to yin, causing everything to happen: just as things expand and contract, and temperatures change from hot to cold. **These two energetic processes can be extended to foods, cooking styles, diagnosing health conditions, looking at a person's nature, physical activity, body organs, just about everything.**

You must be wondering how ancient Chinese philosophy is related to food, and how all of this is supposed to make you beautiful. But have patience, and you'll be rewarded with gems of wisdom, which can change your entire outlook towards eating.

The food you eat, too, has innate energies. It's only that we choose not to see it. Let's start with a simple example.

It's the dead of summer and you go out for a swim. When you get back home, you find yourself gulping down bottles of water because your body fluids have dried up. If you don't drink enough, you'll find yourself dehydrated, and possibly with dry skin the next day (ever noticed how your heels tend to crack during the summer months?). This will soon lead to a contracted condition, resulting in a dry digestive system, which may lead to constipation. This is termed as a **yang** condition. You will need fluids, i.e. **yin**, to balance you out. Yin here being water.

The chart below gives you an idea of yin and yang with regard to foods:

Yang Foods	Yin Foods
Heavy, hard, dense	Light
Grow downwards	Grow upwards
Fibrous, dry, warm, cooked	Wet, cool, raw,
Meaty, salty, stay fresh longer	Spicy, sweet, juicy, oily, perish faster
Dry, cool, thick, slowly growing vegetables such as tubers	Thick, rapidly growing vegetables

So very simply, yang seeks yin and yin seeks yang to balance you out.

The Beauty Diet is rooted in the principles of Traditional Chinese Medicine (TCM) and a yogic diet—both Eastern philosophies. Nutritional balance from an Eastern perspective is very different from how it is perceived in the West. Modern nutrition science is based on knowing the chemical composition of foods and the biochemical workings of the body. Western nutritionists quantify nutrients such as protein, carbohydrates, and fat, then group foods accordingly, with a one-size-fits-all serving recommendation. However, Eastern knowledge goes down to the basics, the root of all things and finds solutions which cater to the individual requirement.

The Food Pyramid

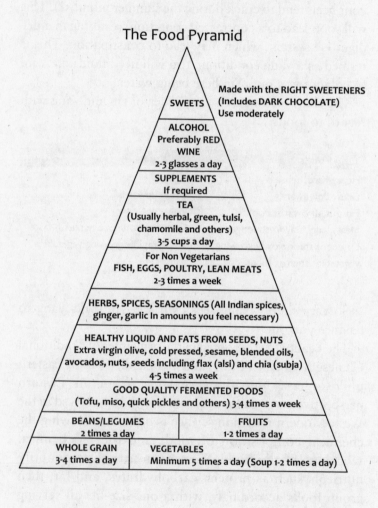

SWEETS — Made with the RIGHT SWEETENERS (Includes DARK CHOCOLATE) Use moderately

ALCOHOL Preferably RED WINE 2-3 glasses a day

SUPPLEMENTS If required

TEA (Usually herbal, green, tulsi, chamomile and others) 3-5 cups a day

For Non Vegetarians FISH, EGGS, POULTRY, LEAN MEATS 2-3 times a week

HERBS, SPICES, SEASONINGS (All Indian spices, ginger, garlic In amounts you feel necessary)

HEALTHY LIQUID AND FATS FROM SEEDS, NUTS Extra virgin olive, cold pressed, sesame, blended oils, avocados, nuts, seeds including flax (alsi) and chia (subja) 4-5 times a week

GOOD QUALITY FERMENTED FOODS (Tofu, miso, quick pickles and others) 3-4 times a week

BEANS/LEGUMES 2 times a day

FRUITS 1-2 times a day

WHOLE GRAIN 3-4 times a day

VEGETABLES Minimum 5 times a day (Soup 1-2 times a day)

For example, the food pyramid, according to Western study, groups bread, pasta, grains, and potatoes together as 'carbohydrates', and suggests five to eight servings. However, according to TCM, bread and pasta are damp and cooling, and thus are not recommended for someone overweight, bloated, or suffering from sinus congestion. Instead it recommends other carbohydrates such as sprouted grains, rye, and wild rice, which do not contribute to dampness because they have energetic properties different from flour and can actually be helpful for people with such yin conditions. Here, the approach varies from person to person.

'Let food be thy medicine, and medicine be thy food.' Now, it's easier to understand this assumption. You can actually use foods to balance you and change your energy or the way you feel. You just need to know how. The living energy (see p 115) in foods is the sum total of everything that has contributed to its growth, i.e. how the food grows, where it grows, the season in which it grows, and how it is treated in cooking when it is used after it grows.

Using this philosophy of energy in foods, my task is to get you off the giant wheel of consuming too much sugar, meats, dairy, and get on the healthy boat of whole grains, beans, vegetables, nuts, seeds, and healthy fats. The change in your craving will soon show itself. And as the cravings for the bad stuff decrease, you will see your body change, skin glow, hair grow, and have a calm, beautiful mind. With all the information in this book, you can get on that surfboard and cruise your own course, no matter how strong the wind.

3

FIVE GROUND RULES

What the Beauty Diet does is look at eating in a more holistic fashion. It understands the secrets behind everything you're putting in your mouth, and whether it's necessary for you or not. But all this information will go to waste if we don't start right at the beginning—which are the fundamentals of where to source your food from, how to eat, and what to eat.

Here's where I simplify things for you. I have five ground rules before we get into the diet you need to follow. And follow you must if you want to go down that beauty path. These rules are the foundation to a great lifestyle.

The Five Ground Rules

RULE 1: GO LOCAL

Walk into the vegetable section of any supermarket and you'll find them, your vegetables, that is, looking like they have travelled the breadth of the country fighting disease and deprivation. These places are the graveyard of vegetables. You should know for a fact that pre-packaged and pre-weighed produce has been in transit or cold stored for days or weeks during which their nutritional value has declined considerably. This also affects the taste of your food. You might as well nibble on an old shoe. Better to get them from the sabziwalla who patrols his rickety cart in your neighbourhood or from the one nestled between the Mother Dairy store and the florist. Chances are he'll have fresher and healthier produce.

Going local will automatically mean that you're eating seasonal produce.

It's the height of summer and you're peeling an orange for yourself. Refreshing, you'd say. But you need to toss that away immediately. That orange is a dead fruit now. Have you ever seen your local sabziwalla selling parwal in winter? I don't think so. And if he is, then you should know that it's not fresh. The benefits of eating what's in season are manifold. Look at the French. A mere 10 percent of French adults are obese, compared with Britain's 22 percent, and America's 33 percent. The French also have higher longevity rates. And it's all because they're dead serious about what they eat. They take pride in their local produce and only eat what's in season. You wear what's in season so why not apply that to what you eat? So in the summer stick to your gourds and pumpkins, which are high in water content and replenish all the water you're losing through the sweltering months. And load your plate with the rich array of cauliflowers, carrots, broccoli, and beans in cold winter months.

We enjoy four seasons: winter (January and February), summer (March to May), a monsoon (rainy) season (June to September), and a post-monsoon period (October to December). So can we eat the same way and use the same cooking styles in all seasons? Not really. When I meet someone who tells me 'I do a raw salad everyday of the year', I can't help but think to myself how damaging that could actually be in winter, especially a winter in the North of India, or when someone says that they cook meat (any meat) daily at one meal, how they are damaging their systems during a hot summer.

This happens because meat is a yang food and produces a drying, contracted effect on the body, and coupled with the summer heat it is a lethal combination, drying you out even further. So meat consumption on a daily basis in the peak of summer should either be balanced with a healthy dose of greens or kept to a minimum. It's in keeping with the theory of climatic change in temperatures and how your body will respond at that particular time.

We all know that a classic remedy for flu is chicken soup (for non vegetarians) and shira, made with sooji, for vegetarians. Why do these work? For starters, chicken, being meat, is warming and will cure a damp condition caused by the flu. The same goes for shira which, when roasted, gives out warm energy to the preparation; adding dry fruits to it will further increase the heat.

Eating seasonally also means you'll be spending less money because unseasonal vegetables usually cost more. ☺

And whoever said that eating local and what's in season is boring? Some of the greatest chefs in the world will tell you the same. It's not just food for food's sake. You should make every meal a culinary adventure.

> 'I passionately believe that our food choices should be ethical, sustainable, and supportive of both the human and natural environment. To cook beautiful meals, you don't need exotic ingredients, just fresh food and flavour—as nature intended. And food is very sensual; it's a whole visual package.'
>
> KYLIE KWONG (CHEF AND RESTAURATEUR)

Plus, you'll be strengthening your local economy and protecting the environment because locally grown food does not travel very far. Next time, think twice before reaching out for those shiny apples from New Zealand.

#Tip: Never hoard your refrigerator with a lifetime's supply of veggies. Buy what you need for the day, or two days if you're too busy to go veggie shopping everyday. Or ask your sabziwalla to come around to your door at a particular time and pick up what you need. And give him a tip in the beginning, he'll definitely show up the next time around.

RULE 2: GO TRADITIONAL

When I was growing up, I remember most of my meals were home-cooked. Eating out was rare and reserved mostly for special occasions. Indians love their food, perhaps more than any other nation in the world, and have a variety to choose from different parts of the country. So families up until a decade ago still stuck to traditional ways of eating. However, with the Indian economy booming, there has been the inevitable advent of American fast-food chains as well as processed foods from the West. As a result, we have started moving away from our traditional diet and are eating out much more than before. Also, fast food is easy, and trendy, as are packaged foods, and most people find these an easier option than home-cooked meals. We are slowly becoming exactly like the Americans—a nation of processed-food eaters. And I don't have to tell you that we're going the unhealthy way, increasing the risk of heart diseases more than ever before.

By going traditional I mean staying away from modern-day high-stress foods, like processed foods, artificial sweeteners, sugars, butter, dairy, high-fructose corn syrup, white bread, fats (trans fats, hydrogenated), soft drinks and beverages loaded with caffeine and other additives, and packaged meats. Traditional nutrition was always centred on whole grains, vegetables, beans, fish, organic meats, organic dairy, nuts, seeds, and fruit. The standard Indian diet of dals, vegetables, and roti is very healthy and works well in the Indian scenario.

> **#Tip:** If you are eating out, try and stick to basic rotis, dal and a vegetable (especially a leafy green), or fish. If you want Continental, then wholewheat pasta (not bread) with a tomato-based sauce. Skip the white sauce with butter and maida and other junk made of refined simple carbs. This way, you will fare better, and keep true to the 'Go Traditional' rule too.

Rule 3: Cooking Styles

Okay, so you eat seasonal vegetables and fruits only. But did you know that the same concept can also be applied to cooking styles? Food and cooking styles, if combined intelligently, have their own energy and thereby the power to influence your energy. If we apply the same yin and yang forces to our cooking, we will see the following:

- Steaming, boiling, and sautéing are an upward rising energy, so they would be a yin style of cooking.
- Pressure cooking, slow cooking, pickling, grilling, and baking produces an inward energy, so they would be a yang style of cooking.

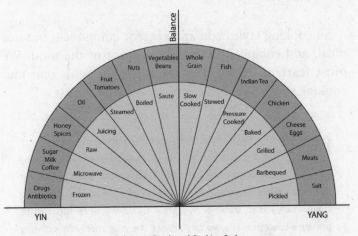

Balance in Foods and Cooking Styles

The chart above shows us that certain foods, when cooked with a particular style, produce an effect which varies from yin to yang. We must learn to find a balance with this. Here are a few pointers:

1) Stronger cooking styles, like pickling, barbequing, grilling, and baking, are more yang as they produce an inward energy and will warm you up, and should therefore be used judiciously during the summer months.

2) If the above styles are used during the summer, they should ideally be counteracted with the more yin styles like steaming, boiling, and sautéing to make for a balanced meal.

3) On the other hand, in the monsoon months, stewing and slow cooking are best coupled with slightly stronger methods, like perhaps grilling or pressure cooking that will also give you warming inward energy.

So cooking styles add an energetic component to your meal, and enhance the health quotient of the food. We must learn to combine seasonal foods with seasonal cooking styles to get the best out of what we eat.

Every Indian household swears by its pressure cookers. They are fuss free and quick. However, pressure cooking produces a yang, or contracted, inward effect. Great for the cold winter months, but too much of an inward energy in a languorous Indian summer will slow us down. Since most of us pressure cook our dals, we can balance the yang energy by sautéing, blanching, or boiling our other foods to release some of that contractedness and encouraging our energy to move up or out. So if you do end up pressure cooking your dal and rice, then sautéing some carrots or greens would be a perfect way to balance this out.

#Tip: Try using different cooking methods at any given meal as a varied number of cooking styles enhances the phytonutrients in the food.

Rule 4: Eating Correctly

There was a time, not very long ago, when children at boarding schools were asked to maintain pin-drop silence while eating. but there was a good reason behind it. The idea behind keeping silent while eating is so that you can concentrate and reflect on what you are eating. However, those are days of yore. What we have now is a mad blur of activity where eating has become secondary, let alone eating silently or while we are stationary. 'To go' are two words which are probably leading to more health issues and weight problems than anything else. Our lives are more hectic than our grandparents' because we seek to compress much more into the 24 hours that we have. In the process, we also lose our balance. However, as human beings seek balance all the time, our bodies react to it by throwing up ailments such as minor coughs and colds, migraine, pains, irritable bowel syndrome, etc. The way you eat reflects things about you as a person. You want to make sure you eat with freedom and no restrictions, so there is no denying yourself. Be mindful of your food, knowing that you are not eating certain foods, as they will not do you any good.

Here's where I turn into a strict matron. When you eat chaotically, and by this I mean skipping meals too, the body wonders why you are treating it this way and is threatened by how you behave towards it. Its defence mechanism hangs onto the fat in your body, slowing down your metabolism, which will cause ailments in the long run. **We need to eat in peace. Period. No talking on the phone. No watching the telly. No pottering about with a slice of pizza in one hand. Find a spot, sit, and eat your food like we were always meant to.** The more organized you are in your eating habits, the more likely it is that you will be in control of your weight, health condition, and how your food is assimilated after the meal.

Set aside a meal time, be regular, and sit down to eat

According to Traditional Chinese Medicine (TCM), each organ has its own peak activity time (see picture on next page). The stomach's time is 7 to 9 am, which should be breakfast time. Similarly, the stomach's minimum activity time is 12 hours away from it peak time of 7 to 9 pm. Any time between or after noon to 1.00 pm should be lunch, which should be your largest meal. This varies if you are only going to eat two meals a day, i.e. breakfast and dinner, then make breakfast larger than dinner. However, Indians are used to a three-meal schedule, i.e. breakfast, lunch, and dinner, and in the morning there should be an hour at least after rising before eating so that the body and organs can gradually adjust to active states of energy. It is usually good to eat, once the body sends you a sign of hunger. In such a case, breakfast should be a smaller meal compared to lunch, while dinner should be before 7 pm, and it must be a small meal if you go to bed between 10 and 10.30 pm. The further away from the liver's peak activity time a meal is taken (which is 1 am to 3 am), the better the liver will perform its job. In most cases people eat a late dinner, which puts a burden on the liver and interferes with its other jobs, specially blood purification which is its most important job and vital to maintain good health and blood condition.

Organ Activity Time

Of course, it may be difficult to adhere to these timings, and you have to work out what's best for you. But sticking to timings is the key for assimilation by a particular body organ.

Just sit, will you. I cannot emphasize how important sitting down and eating a meal is to achieve any kind of balance—whether you are trying to lose weight, work with diabetes, thyroid, or any other health issue. It will encourage you to be more present, and chew well, and it gets you to spend time with the family. Meal times should be treated like a sacred ritual.

Remember, your body bathes in nutrients when fed calmly. Okay, let me make it more attractive for you—you can actually lose weight by eating correctly. Intrigued now, are we?

5 reasons why you should be eating slowly

1) **Control weight gain:** When you eat slowly, you tend to consume fewer calories. The reason is that it takes about twenty minutes for our brains to register that we're full. If we eat fast, we can continue eating past the point where we're full. If we eat slowly, we have time to realize we're full, and stop on time.

2) **Better digestion:** When you eat slowly, you chew your food better, which leads to better digestion. Digestion actually starts in the mouth; so the more work you do up there, the less you'll have to do in your stomach.

3) **Enjoy your food:** What's the point of eating if you don't even relish your food? Turn off that TV, switch off your phone, and pay attention to what you're eating. It'll make you happy.

4) **Less stress:** Eating slowly, and paying attention to our food, can be a great form of mental exercise. Be in the moment, rather than rushing through a meal thinking about what you need to do next. This will lead to a less stressful life.

5) **Catch up:** There's a reason we have meal times. This is the time when a family actually sits down together.

It improves relationships and is a great bonding time. Plus you can catch up on all the gossip about your neighbours. So don't take your food to your room the next time.

> ### THE ART OF CHEWING
>
> Your mouth secretes an enzyme called ptyalin, which needs to be mixed well with the food to aid digestion. Complex carbohydrates break down in the mouth first, releasing its sugars (and other vitamins and minerals) to be absorbed by your system. Plus, your saliva is alkaline, which in turn alkalizes the food. If you don't chew your food, you will develop flatulence and end up feeling heavy, disoriented, and bloated. You can make your digestion easy by chewing which brings about lightness in you and your body. So, if you want to shed the weight, CHEW!

RULE 5: VARY YOUR MEALS

When clients first come to me, I make them write at the end of the evaluation booklet of the food they eat—from the time they wake up to the time they go to bed. This gives me an indication of how they are eating, and their cravings and addictions as far as food is concerned. Many clients eat just vegetables and rotis every single day, while some skip the grain component completely in all their meals to keep their weight off. Forty-year-old Rajiv has been my client for a while. When he first came to me, Rajiv's diary of food habits revealed that he ate pretty much the same thing everyday, day in and day out. His afternoon and evening meals also had not changed much over the years. When I asked him, he told me that he had eaten toast and eggs or muesli for breakfast for the past fifteen years of his life! What he didn't realize, till I pointed it out, was that he had become a creature of habit. It was also one of the reasons he was constantly struggling with some illness or the other and not losing any weight.

Meal times are not just about eating anything, but actually about eating intelligently so as to be nourished by what you eat. If you eat the same food day in and day out, your body gets used to it and becomes dull, especially if the food is processed and straight out of a box. Doing this also means that you are missing out on a whole range of other nutrients which are essential for you. The goal is to use a variety of cooking styles, ingredients, and foods. This increases the ability of the body to absorb the various nutrients and to affect your state of mind and your moods. A new flavour or taste is a treat for your body which wakes up to understand and assimilate this new element, just as your brain becomes dull if you keep doing the same work for long periods of time. You have a whole range of grains, vegetables, and fish to choose from, so why stick to just what you know? Love your food, experiment, try new things.

#Tip: Make sure your food always has texture and colour. You can do this for a soup by using upto 2 tbs of brown rice in 2 cups of soup and blending it into the soup to give it a grainy texture. For colour, steam the vegetable you are using to make a soup and blend these separately to add colour. For example, you can do this with broccoli soup—the steaming action makes it green and once blended, it will add colour to the soup.

IN A NUTSHELL...

- 'You are what you eat' because the foods you eat go a step beyond just tasting good and satisfying your taste buds; they help nourish you and find their own levels when they make their way into your body.
- Each living food has its own energy, prana or life force, as we Indians say. This life force also influences the life force within each of us. We use the life force in foods to change our own life force.
- Eat seasonal.
- Meal times are sacred. Take time out for them.
- Vary your food and cooking styles across seasons to change the way you feel.

Now let's focus on foods that will keep us healthy for life. **Let's go beyond the diet to a lifestyle plan.** Stop counting calories, restricting portions, going on raw and juice fasts, or eating sweets with guilt. Let's feed the body with food that nourishes it and helps it to function on a different level with strength and vitality. Also, use the same food to reduce the risks of future ailments, strengthen the immune system, give you that glow, great head of hair and slow down the ageing process. Let's use food as a medicine every day, and in the most exciting way to be beautiful.

4

WHAT NOT TO EAT

If you're yawning at the chapter title thinking, 'yeah, yeah I already know what not to eat...the fried stuff, the jalebis', you're well...partially wrong. Messages about what we should and shouldn't eat bombard us on a daily basis. So what are we to believe?

Sure you need to keep your hands off that samosa, and yes, you can't get yourself a combo box of doughnuts from that heaven-sent store that's right on your street, but there's more. Oh no! you think. And this time you're right. There's much more on that list that does us nothing but harm, and we need to identify those culprits immediately. Furthermore, your body is perpetually changing. So what is best for you now might be different from your ideal diet ten years from now. Some of our food habits have been around for so long that we take it for granted that they work for us. Five decades ago, wearing crocodile-skin shoes and a mink fur coat was uber cool; yet today they're symbols of cruelty and violation, and we consciously stay away from such things. What if we could do the same with our food and question the accepted food culture that's been passed on to us? What I'm going to do in this chapter is break down some of those food-related myths.

1) Say no to dairy

G, also called Gurnoor, has her feet propped up on the coffee table and is channel surfing when she stops at an advertisement for a fairness cream. 'Gah,' she scowls in disdain, 'such rubbish. Look at me, I've never used a cream on my face, forget about fairness cream and see…fair, supple skin, and never a pimple. It's all that milk and dahi I drink and, of course, my Punjabi genes. Rubbish all these ads are.'

G is both right and wrong. Right about her genes, and wrong about the dairy diet. But I dare not mention it to her right then, seeing how flared up she already was about the ad playing on TV. In fact, this is such a controversial topic among Indians that I have reached a point of not bringing it up at all when I am out because the discussion gets pretty heated after a while. Let's face it, as Indians we love our dairy. We stick up for dairy as if it's our best friend; the excuses are innumerable and range from it being comfort food, and the diet of our ancestors, to it being a source of calcium, necessary for strength, shiny hair, and much more.

As the product of a north Indian household, my dairy consumption per day must have easily been 1 litre while I was growing up. I remember our domestic help chasing after me to the school bus stop with a glass of milk. To add to the milk, there was yoghurt, which we had to eat at lunch time, and paneer, cheese, and oh so much more! Did it make me any stronger, or my skin fairer, or creamier? I don't think it did. What I do know is that I saw a sea change in my body shape after I quit dairy completely. I got leaner, the fat around my thighs vanished, my hips got narrower, and my stomach was never ever bloated. Here's the truth. We don't need dairy as much as we think we do. Dairy is classified as animal food. John McDougall, MD, author and nutrition expert, says dairy products can cause issues ranging from digestive disorders, premenstrual symptoms, allergies, bronchial issues, breast cancer, to autoimmune disorders, and has linked them to over forty five other diseases. Frank Oski, author of *Don't Drink Your Milk*, states that milk alters the human body, and considers it a hazardous food.

Why, would be the next question.

Milk is energetically and hormonally meant for a baby to bond with the mother, and this ends once a child is weaned off the mother's breast. It is our first association with food and therefore a tough one to give up, as it makes for comfort food.

Your lungs and large intestines work as a team when it comes to processing milk in the body. We all know that the lungs receive oxygen and eliminate carbon dioxide. Lactase is an enzyme found in the small intestine and its primary function is to breakdown lactose (the sugar in milk) into simple sugars. It is particularly abundant during infancy, after which it starts decreasing, especially after the age of four. When milk is ingested in large quantities, the amount of lactose is greater than the lactase in the digestive system. The reason behind it is the natural concept of absorption.

Here's a simple example. Take a glass of water and add salt to it. The salt will definitely dissolve. Now keep adding more and more, and soon you'll reach a point where the water will reach its maximum absorption point and will not be able to dissolve any more salt. It's the same with dairy or anything in excess. The excess milk will simply accumulate in this region, where it will ferment and react with the existing bacteria in your gut. The fermented excess will then convert to carbon dioxide and lactic acid, which builds up water pressure in all your tissues. Your lungs receive oxygen and eliminate carbon dioxide, an excess of which produces acidic blood, which will slow you down and also create mental fatigue. Acidic blood is like sludge (mucky and thick). This makes the flow of it difficult and slows down the organs.

Go back to our ancestors, to the cave man. The only time a person would ever ingest lactose would be when they were infants, getting milk from their mothers. Thereafter in their lives, milk was never consumed. It's only with the invention of agriculture and animal husbandry that milk became readily available to adults. We weren't made to be dairy eaters. Take a pointer from it.

7 reasons why dairy is bad for you:

1) Dairy is high in saturated fats, predisposing us to cholesterol deposits in the arteries. As explained earlier, the fat in dairy accumulates in the body,

adding bulky layers over your muscle. This fat build-up hinders and slows down oxygen from reaching other body tissues surrounding it. And a lack of oxygen slows your metabolism, making your system sluggish and eventually adding weight to your body.

2) According to *The China Study* by T. Colin Campbell, casein is a protein that does not assimilate in the digestive system, and dairy has plenty of it. Cow's milk has 18 percent whey and 40 percent casein. Think of casein going into your tummy and becoming like curd, which sticks to your intestinal walls. This interferes with the digestive system's ability to absorb nutrients from other foods, causing fat deposits.

3) Typically, deposits in soft tissue stick around and can get malignant over time. That's why incidences of cancers, and especially breast cancer, has increased in India. Women who consume a diet rich in animal-based foods, with a reduced amount of plant-based foods, reach puberty earlier and menopause later, thus extending their reproductive lives. They also have higher levels of female hormones (which includes estrogen) throughout their lifespan. A lifetime's exposure to estrogen exposes women to be at high risk to breast cancer. Diet plays a major role in establishing estrogen exposure. Increased level of estrogen exposure and related hormones are a result of the consumption of typical Western diets, high in fat and animal protein, and low in dietary fibre. Cow's milk protein is an exceptionally potent cancer promoter. In an experiment conducted by

The China Study, casein, which makes up for 87 percent of cow's milk, was used on rats and promoted cancer on initiation. Most women who have had breast cancer, have been heavy dairy consumers.

4) Lactase remains in the intestine up until about one year of age, after which it begins to dwindle. After four years of age, it no longer exists, making digestion of milk difficult. Most people don't know this and live with acid reflux and digestive issues all their lives, but still continue consuming dairy products.

5) Milk's pH balance is 6.5, making it slightly acidic. When consumed it is further warmed in our body, increasing acidity levels. This creates a home for bad bacteria to thrive in, impacting your immune system negatively. If you have mucous-related issues such as candida, discharges from the nose, asthma, allergies, sinus, or other problems such as constipation, excess weight, bad skin, or a thick-coated white tongue, you may want to cut back the dairy in your diet. My candida issue (discussed later) came about because of excessive milk as a child.

6) Pasteurization (the heating of milk usually done before packing to kill the bacteria in it it for the consumer) causes loss of important vitamins and destroys beneficial enzymes and also alters calcium levels in milk. Homogenization (treating milk to break the fat in milk into smaller sizes, so it does not rise up or separate, and the consumer gets evenly-separated milk) increases the chances of milk putrefying and causing oxidation in the body, creating newer fat membranes with higher casein.

Also, homogenization releases an enzyme called xanthine oxidase in your blood, which damages membranes, causing scar tissue (wound) wherein cholesterol accumulates and clogs arteries when it enters the heart and arteries. Vitamin D plays a key role in the utilization of calcium in the body. Due to this reason, the dairy industry fortifies its milk with synthetic forms of Vitamin D (calciferol). Magnesium stimulates calcitonin (hormone) production, which increases calcium in the bones and keeps it from being absorbed in the tissues of the body. However, the synthetic version of Vitamin D in fortified milk removes magnesium from the body. Hence, while we need magnesium to absorb calcium, fortified Vitamin D milk ends up depleting magnesium stores. So of what good is the Vitamin D, when we don't have the magnesium to absorb it? And without magnesium, how will cacitonin production take place to increase calcium in our bones? So therefore, just because calcium exists in milk, it does not necessarily mean you can absorb it. A major proportion of people in the world do not rely on dairy for their calcium needs, and still end up having strong bones and teeth. Like me!

7) Cows are given growth hormones to increase the production of milk. When we drink milk, we also end up consuming some of these hormones because cow's milk is referred to as 'unstructured tissue' by Steve Gagne about the energetics of milk. Since your body does not have the capacity to process this 'unstructured tissue', the casein in it bonds with your

tissue and is likely to negatively influence them. Since I'm dairy free, if I eat a small piece of cheese, I know the difference in my body tissue within a couple of hours—my stomach sticks out instantly, and my love handles pad up. It's amazing how quickly a body reacts.

The calcium and dairy myth

The next logical question that you will ask is, 'If I don't drink milk, where will I get my calcium from.' We've always been told to drink milk as it strengthens our bones. But if dairy is consumed because of the calcium theory, then why is it that after a point, a baby calf weans off its mother's milk (just as we human's do), but still has big bones and produces milk in its turn? Where do they get their calcium from? The answer is that cow's get their calcium from the grass (rich in chlorophyll and magnesium) that they eat.

The calcium in milk is bonded to casein. And casein, as you now know, is not easily absorbed in the body. Only 12 percent of calcium can be used by the body, the rest remains undigested. Caesin accumulates undigested in the upper intestine, producing toxins, and leading to a weakening of body systems and an increase in mucous deposits. The body then attempts to isolate this excess by creating cysts and tumours. In addition, these deposits can accumulate in the kidney and gall bladder, leading to stones. And since dairy consumption also creates an overtly acidic condition in the body, it starts eating into what is known as 'serum calcium' (the little calcium in your blood and bones). So while marketers tout that dairy is giving you the calcium, they refuse to mention that what you are also getting is the casein which, when undigested, leaches calcium from the bones. People also get osteoporosis because they are having other stuff which is stripping them off the calcium in their body, such as colas, coffee, sugar, dairy, meat, and tobacco, and not due to a lack of calcium. Lack of exercise and a high stress lifestyle are also major factors. So in the process of trying to get calcium from dairy, we, in fact, are creating an accumulation of excess calcium, which is harmful for us.

Another thing. Calcium needs cofactors such as magnesium, and Vitamin C and D to assimilate. People suffering from osteoarthritis, a joint disorder, should add magnesium-rich foods to their diet. Some magnesium-rich foods are spirulina (as the chlorophyll has magnesium in its centre and helps absorb calcium), wheat grass, soybeans, and their byproducts—tofu, miso, whole beans, especially moong, black beans, grains (millet, corn, barley, and brown rice), and sesame seeds. Of course, nuts and seeds are always a good addition (see Recipe section for a condiment for your table). You need calcium from different sources, the most if you have heart disease, bone disorders, high blood pressure, nervous system problems, in growing years (adolescent and childhood), and women post menopause.

Absorbable calcium for your body actually comes from leafy greens, nut seeds, beans, and whole grains. Substitute dairy with chlorophyll or magnesium-rich foods such as spirulina, kombu (available at some speciality stores), and barley/wheat grass. These are superfoods, rich in not only magnesium, but all trace minerals, better sources of calcium, and excellent for bone-related issues. So stay off the dairy as much as you can. And the next time you hear someone saying, 'Drink that, it's good for you', you can tell them otherwise.

KNOW YOUR CALCIUM

CALCIUM DEPLETERS

1. Alcohol, marijuana, cigarettes, and other intoxicants.
2. Excess of animal food protein and protein in general.
3. Sugar or too much of any concentrated sweetener.
4. Coffee and soft drinks.
5. Too little or too much exercise.
6. Excess salt.
7. Vegetables: Minimize tomatoes, potatoes, (not sweet potatoes), eggplant, and bell peppers, which contain solanine in the skin (an alkaloid which is toxic and cannot be destroyed by cooking).

SOURCES OF CALCIUM

1. Eating calcium, magnesium, and chlorophyll-rich foods such as grain, leafy greens, and beans.
2. Presoak all beans and grains. This helps with the phytic acid content which will inhibit absorption of calcium and magnesium.
3. Use fermented dairy instead of dairy.
4. Sit out in the morning sun for thirty minutes for your daily dose of Vitamin D for better calcium absorption.
5. Exercise, exercise, exercise!

Can't give it up? Here are a few alternatives:

1) Use full fat, raw milk, and milk products. Ask your milkman. Chances are, he'll be able to give you full-fat unpasteurized milk. At least that's a starter.

2) Do not make milk and milk products the 'main characters' in your diet; give them supporting roles instead.

DID YOU KNOW?

Cheese creates a dry condition in the body and adds to wrinkling of the skin when eaten in excess; while excessive butter creates a damp effect and restricts blood flow to the brain, and causes sluggishness in the body.

3) If you use pasteurized milk, remember to first boil and cool it. Boiling milk breaks down the protein chains, and makes them easier to assimilate (making it also safer for infants). Pasteurization takes place at a temperature below boiling, so it only breaks the protein chains partially. If you are using pasteurized milk, a quick boil will finish the protein chain breakdown.

WHAT ABOUT SKIMMED MILK?

'I drink only skimmed milk, because I don't want to put on weight. So why the fuss?' Most weight-conscious people think that skimmed milk is a better option since the fat has been removed but the essential vitamins have been retained. Let me tell you this:

skimmed milk is like drinking water as there is nothing there of any benefit to you. You will actually lose more minerals by having it regularly because it is a derivative of milk, and waste for the body. It does not assimilate, leading to cysts, and your skin will show this as well with a change in colour. Switch to whole raw milk instead.

4) A person who is lactose intolerant should only drink fermented milk products such as yoghurt, buttermilk (chaas), and paneer. And people with yeast infections and candida should avoid all dairy products, including yoghurt, as it causes more dampness in the body.

5) Make your own milk at home (see Recipe section).

These alternatives are more nutritious and are minus the baggage that comes with regular milk.

IS SOY MILK A GOOD SUBSTITUTE?

Soy milk is being touted as a good source of protein, and most people who give up milk immediately switch to soy milk as a substitute. But it comes with its downside. After soy milk is processed, it loses its goodness and does not have the same benefits as whole soybean. Soybeans contain potent enzyme-inhibitors. These inhibitors block uptake of enzymes which the body needs for protein digestion. The kidneys have a hard time flushing it out of your system. Soy milk also builds up sludge in the system, and can leave you feeling bloated and gassed up.

Limit your intake to fermented soy products like miso and tofu as fermenting deactivates these enzymes and makes digestion easier. And for people trying to lose weight, these things are best avoided completely.

2) There's poison and then there is sugar

Except that poison kills faster and death by sugar is slow and comes with additional complications. And here in India, there's no escaping it. We have to face it; India has a sweet tooth with a bite to kill. Some would argue that it's more like an addiction. Sugar is everywhere. A meal is always ended with a bit of (you wish it were just a bit) halwa, fruit, or a barfi. And this is despite the fact that we're also consuming it in other forms soft drinks, candy, cake, cookies, ice cream, bottled teas, coffee drinks, etc. To add to this exhausting list there are the hidden sugars, the guerillas, tucked away in places you'll never guess, such as salad dressings, soups, breads, pizzas, pasta sauce, salsa, and even bottled water. Whether in the form of white sugar, high fructose corn syrup, cane juice, or honey, **too much sugar is too much sugar**. Sugar is the wily devil, tempting, clever, and addictive as hell.

Here's my story. My only living grandparent was my grandmother from my maternal side. She never had a regular dinner made for her kids, ending their day with high tea instead. Their 'high tea' consisted of a whole lot of junk processed food such as pastries, cookies, sandwiches, and milk. Children's food habits are shaped within the first seven years, so my grandmother had set her kids up for an eternal sweet tooth. My mother can still have something sweet after breakfast, lunch, and dinner and in between meals and at teatime, which is pretty much around the clock. As I grew up, I noticed that mother had a lot of anger and would lose her cool pretty often, in fits and bursts throughout the day. Of course she put it down to the three of us (my brother, sister, and me), but when I finally understood the mystery behind sugar, I knew I had found the culprit.

A couple of years ago, my mother started complaining of aching bones. By then I was well on my way to being a macrobiotic counsellor and was aware of how sugar works in the system. Her calcium levels and bone density tests were fine, and technically there was nothing wrong with her. A very eminent orthopaedic diagnosed it as degenerative changes in the body and recommended steroids if the pain got worse. I analysed her situation and everything pointed in the direction of a Vitamin B12 deficiency—she is an ovo vegetarian (she has eggs and dairy), so logically she should have had B12 stores. However, I knew that copious amounts of sugar deplete those Vitamin B12 stores in the body, causing severe bone pain. I suggested that she do a Vitamin B12 test. She tested positive with a deficiency of B12. For a cure, I simply added glucosamine (a compound found naturally in the body, which is depleted with age and is much needed to maintain healthy cartilage) to her list of supplements and B12. She is fine now, but, of course, still refuses to give up sugar. She has mood swings, although reduced, but I love her anyway, with or without the sugar.

No nutritionist taught me the meaning of hidden sugars in foods that I bought off the shelf. I loved my granola bars, bread, and diet coke. And I generally trusted anything that said 'sugar free' or 'fat free'. I never read labels at the back of a package and never knew the difference between simple and complex sugars, and continued eating what I thought was healthy. The problem with sugars is that they are so widespread and included in so many things that it's very difficult to avoid them. Hence we are going through this lesson on sugar to learn how to beat it at its own game.

Let's jog your memory on what simple sugars do. Sugar once eaten is quickly absorbed by your body and spikes your blood-sugar levels. It's a bit of a shock to your body—your pancreas secretes insulin to drop your blood-sugar levels back to normal. That's why you feel that sugar high (insulin burst) and then a crash—what we term as the **sugar blues**. Therefore, what you are essentially doing is exhausting your metabolism and also adding to your fat cells. This spike and crash routine is bad for a few reasons:

- Makes you sick: it suppresses your immune response
- Makes you fat: it makes you crave food and increases your calorie consumption once the insulin has passed
- Makes you tired: you may feel sleepy after you're sugar high because your body has worked twice as hard to break it down

Other harmful effects of sugar

- It strips minerals over time from your body and more importantly, calcium from your bones, causing osteoporosis and anaemia. Sugar causes cavities, which leads to expensive dental bills. So if not for anything else, avoid sugar to cut cost!
- Since sugar has a dispersing upward energy, it fuels the brain unnecessarily (if had in excess), causing melodrama, anxiety, mood swings, depression, and loss of sleep.

- Low and high sugar levels cause irritability, headaches, and a stripping away of tryptophan (amino acid), which is needed for harmony in the brain. You lose all your B vitamins, and this includes the little stores of B12, causing hair fall as minerals get depleted.
- Sugar also throws off the pH balance in your blood and causes mucous in the system, a perfect place for yeast and bad bacteria to survive.
- The organs that are most affected by excessive sugar are the spleen and pancreas from where the insulin is activated.

Learn to recognize hidden sugars on labels

It's important that you know what kind of sugar your treat contains. Spot the ones that are nothing but trouble for your body. Here are some of the things you should watch out for while looking at the ingredient list:

1) Stay away from the treat if it contains sucrose, maltose, lactose, glucose, and fructose, or any ingredient with a name that ends with the syllable 'ose'. These are all sugars.

2) Avoid anything with the word corn in it. Corn syrup, corn syrup solids, high-fructose corn syrup, and organic corn syrup. High-fructose corn syrup is a highly refined, artificial product, and is more dangerous than sugar itself, used in food products since the 1980s. It represents more than 40 percent of sweeteners added to food and beverages amongst

packaged products because it is cheap. It is similar to sugar, but much higher in calories. Research indicates that it inhibits the production of leptin—a hormone that lets you know you are full—which then makes you overeat.

3) Look out for sweeteners such as molasses, invert sugar syrup, sorghum syrup, agave nectar, and cane and malt sugar which are all simple sugars, causing the same havoc in the body that sugar would.

ARTIFICIAL SWEETENERS

Artificial sweeteners like aspartame, sucralose, acesulfame K, and saccharin contain chemicals which have long-term effects on the heart and have also been known to cause cancer.

Aspartame has been linked to headaches and to neuropsychiatric disorders like panic attacks, mood changes, hallucinations, and depression.

Saccharin on the other hand has shown to produce wheezing, nausea, diarrhoea, blisters, headaches, and a lot more if consumed over a period of time.

Some sweeteners scream 'no aspartame' in their advertising, but have sucralose, which cause the thymus gland (your key to immunity) to shrink. **Sucralose** will cause problems ranging from disruption of sleep, weight gain, and sexual dysfunction to lupus, degenerative diseases, and cancer. Think of it as ingesting tiny amounts of chlorinated pesticide every time you take a small dose of sweeteners that have sucralose.

Some sweeteners have a blend of aspartame, sucralose, and acesulfame K linked to all types of tumours, leukaemia, and chronic respiratory diseases.

---

4) Watch out for chocolate bars which profess to be **sugar free**. They contain maltitol, xylitol, erythritol, and sugar alcohols, which are used to replace sugar because they have fewer calories. Although they are highly refined, they can still ferment in the intestines and cause bloating, gas, or diarrhoea.

5) As for the term 'no added sugar', it means that no sugar (processed sugar such as sucrose) was added to the foods that naturally contain sugar. For example, jams, jellies, other preservatives, milk, and tomato sauce, have quite a bit of natural sugar (fructose) in it so they don't require any more sugar. The term 'no added sugar' just makes it sound like a healthier option. So don't touch that diet drink!

6) Anything processed or in a can will definitely have sugar.

DIABETES AND SUGAR-FREE PRODUCTS

Diabetes may be the most commonly misunderstood disease. Most people think diabetes is simply a disease which means you just can't eat sugar. The artificial sugar industry markets fake sugars as totally harmless to the diabetic patient, and tempts them into believing they can eat and drink all they want by 'tricking' their bodies.

Are honey and jaggery better than regular sugar?

Indians often believe that honey and jaggery are a better option, when in fact they fall under simple sugars. However, honey has a special enzyme which aids in digesting it a little differently than sugar. Therefore the absorption in the bloodstream is slower than sugar, and it has a lower glycemic index. It is slightly higher in calories than sugar, but it has antioxidant properties. Though honey maybe a safer alternative, it still classifies as a simple sugar. I would recommend alternating it with other healthier options.

Jaggery, on the other hand, is unrefined sugar. It works the same way as sugar does in the body and is not recommended as a substitute to sugar. It has the same calorie content as sugar too. Even though jaggery cleans the lungs, stomach, intestines, esophagus, and respiratory tract, it cannot be consumed as an alternative to sugar.

STEVIA: THE SAFE SUGAR IN INDIA

Stevia is a whole herbal food. It is a plant which grows in Latin America and is now being commercially used all over the world. Besides adding sweetness to food and drinks, it cures mental and physical fatigue, harmonizes digestion, blood pressure, and assists in weight loss as it has zero calories. You get it in power and extract formats. It can also be used by people with candida for whom normal sweeteners are not recommended.

Use it sparingly, as overuse will cause weakness. Stevia does have an aftertaste, so start using smaller amounts at first to build a taste for it. One to three drops of the Stevia extract will sweeten 1 cup of liquid. It can be used in desserts, beverages, tea, coffee, and even baking. It works well for my diabetic patients too.

Be smart with your sugar intake

Remember the balance chart on yin and yang foods, and on not eating from the two extreme ends of the polarity of yin and yang? Well sugar is extremely yin, and yin energy is expansive, so it will expand you, that is, make you gain weight. Also, since yin energies are rising energies, they go up to your brain very quickly, making you irritable, jittery, and angry.

Leaving sugar completely out of our lives is impossible. What you need to do is balance it out. And here's how to do it.

Balancing out sugar

1. Some yang to balance out the yin: The day you decide, or have by chance consumed sugar in any form, make sure you also have something yang (downward energy) to combat it. Make yourself a nice brown rice pulao with plenty of round vegetables and leafy greens thrown in (see Round Vegetables Soup recipe on p 299), eat it with some fish or meat or chicken if you are a non vegetarian.

2. Going out for a drink? Make sure you eat meat or fish (a much better option), and if you are a vegetarian then have some strong cooked curries with vegetables. Consciously stay away from the dessert counter the day you decide to drink.

3. If you are going out for a wedding/party and want to avoid sugar, have a big bowl of brown rice with sweet vegetables as the last meal for the day (see

p 262) or the Sweet Vegetable Drink (see p 306). This will not make you crave sugar at the event.

4. Chew your whole grain, legumes, and vegetables well, as this will release the right sugars required to balance out the levels in your body and give you sustained sugars. Cravings for sugar will decrease, as balanced meals become a part of your daily dietary regimen.

5. Be aware of all the so-called sugars which are referred to as natural such as fructose, brown sugar, maltitol, xylitol, sorbitol, cane and beet sugars, but are not really natural.

6. Sweeten desserts with fruit juice and pulps, stevia, and pure maple syrup (see the Recipe section for ideas).

7. Include sweet vegetables such as carrots, cabbage, onions, and red pumpkin in your dishes almost daily. This way you are getting sugar from a natural source and it will help bring down your sugar cravings.

8. Use sprouts or sprouted products as these convert starch to digestible sugar. The microorganisms that help with the sprouting process predigest starches into sugars, and also give you the right protein to regulate the sugar in your bloodstream.

9. Counteract sugar cravings with sour, spicy, or pungent flavours. These flavours improve the digestive activity of the spleen and pancreas (which act up when there are sugar cravings), thus seeking to quell these sugar cravings. Cravings usually arise due to erratic food habits like eating too much yin foods and then swinging to yang foods or eating

chaotically. This throws the sugar level out of balance, and you end up craving more sugar.

10. Have more home-cooked meals than outside to avoid hidden sugars from foods.

11. Go through the transition slowly, don't quit overnight or minimize by interspersing with ideas recommended.

12. Have chamomile tea with lime to counteract acid reflux, which causes you to crave sugars.

13. Do something to distract your mind for a while till the craving subsides, such as taking deep breaths. Alternately, make yourself a cup of tea with a slice of lemon in it.

Sugar always craves for more sugar. It's one of the tenets of this approach. So how do we get over this addiction? Well, it's like any other addiction—slow and steady. Don't just quit or you will go through extreme withdrawal symptoms. As you start with the above recommendations, you will start replacing the simple sugars with complex sugars more suited for you, and the sugar cravings will gradually decrease.

3) The skinny on fats

We all need fat, but fat can confuse us. It took me a long time to understand where my good fats came from. To use or not to use oil (liquid fats) was the question I faced, before I understood the mechanics behind good fats. There has been so much written about fats and so much controversy around the subject that it can all get very confusing. The fact is that we need fats for a healthy body, normal weight, great skin, and hair. And if you've reduced your fat intake, become a vegetarian, gone off dairy, the need to include quality vegetarian fat increases even more. Some fats promote our health positively while others increase our risk of heart disease. Fat will make you fat if eaten in excess. This also includes liquid fat (the oil you are eating), padding up your hips, thighs, and contributing to cellulite. What you have to learn is which fats you need and the ones you can really do without. And to also rethink the 'no oil in your food' mantra.

If we go back to the balance chart, **fats are yin as they create a sense of security** and heaviness. So for people who are overweight, mentally disturbed, or highly emotional— the wrong fats can worsen these issues. Have you ever wondered why you feel heavy and sluggish after eating a meal which is greasy? This is because your meal was possibly full of saturated fat, which lurks around in your system, making your blood sludgy; so you feel this sluggishness. Fats, when right and when ingested in the human body, gather momentum and become the mechanism that starts transporting nutrients to all your organs; it warms and energizes you (gaining a yang nature). Hence, good oil will make it easier for the body systems to function at its optimum and give you a sense of grounding and make you feel secure.

Fats should be consumed moderately by people who have a high degree of heat in their bodies, which is manifested by redness in the face, bloodshot eyes, high blood pressure, people who have the tendency to feel hot more than others, or people who have candida—yeast in their bodies (explained in Chapter 5)—tumours, cysts, and oedema.

The bad boys of fats: trans fats

You've heard enough about it. But if you haven't paid attention, these are the first types of fats which need to go. Trans fats can be found in all commercially packaged foods—everything from biscuits, cakes, pastries, french fries, chicken nuggets, burgers, pizzas, microwave popcorn, margarine, and a whole lot more, and all the yummy restaurant food. The range is so wide that you invariably end up eating a large dose of trans fats daily. Trans fats should be limited to 2 grams per day in a 2000-calorie diet. Minimize trans fats and saturated fats. We need to get our fats from natural foods and the good quality oils.

CALCULATING HIDDEN TRANS FATS

You can calculate how much hidden trans fat there is in a food packet, especially when it isn't mentioned. Go to the total fats section of the food label, and add up the polyunsaturated, monounsaturated, and saturated fat amounts. If the number is less than the total fats number, the unaccounted part is the trans fats.

Smoking points

Cooking oils and fats react differently to heat. But in general, the hotter they get, the more they break down and eventually start to smoke. Smoke point is the temperature after which different oils begin to break down and become unhealthy. Just remember:

- **The higher the smoke point, the healthier the oil** (canola, ghee, avocado, coconut, mustard, rice bran, extra virgin olive).
- **The lower the smoke point, the unhealthier the oil** (butter, lard, hydrogenated vegetable oil, sunflower, and a low-grade olive oil).

However,

- Certain oils are better for deep frying and sautéing than others (Butter has a low smoke point and is good for sautéing, whereas mustard oil has a high smoke point and is good for deep frying).

Tip#: When deep frying food, dropping little bits of batter or bread into the oil accelerates its breakdown, lowering its smoke point even more. Therefore not making it suitable for frying.

Choosing a healthy oil

The subject of healthy cooking oils is probably one of the most misunderstood subjects in health. The usual recommendation from nutritionists and dietitians is to use polyunsaturated oils such as corn and soybean oil, as well as monounsaturated fats like olive and canola. Polyunsaturated vegetable oils like corn, sunflower, and soybean contain an ingredient called linoleic acid (an essential fatty acid). When heated, as we do in Indian cooking, they become unstable and break down as they are polyunsaturated in nature. This leads to the formation of what we term as 'free radicals' in the body. The essential fatty acids, which should actually help you, are broken down and cause you more harm.

Picture a clean wall (your cell structure) with cracks and holes. Free radicals are the cracks and holes. What you need is a primer (the right antioxidants and the right oil) to fill up these cracks and holes. But what we do instead is keep making more cracks and holes by constantly eating the same oils. With an increase in the cracks and holes, you set the stage for diseases of all sorts to hit you sooner than you can imagine.

Polyunsaturated vegetable oils like flax, sunflower, chia, walnuts, and soybean should be eaten in their raw form and also used raw. Oils which are polyunsaturated in nature are best for salad dressings, but not for cooking. **If at all you wish to use polyunsaturated oils, make sure you buy cold-pressed oils. Do not allow the oil to smoke. That's when it starts to turn bad.**

What do we cook our food in?

Monounsaturated fats are the best for cooking, especially when coupled with some blended oils. These fats are like polyunsaturated fats since they provide EFAs or essential fatty acids which nourish many of the body's functions including maintaining a healthy skin. Many sources of monounsaturated fats are usually good sources of Vitamin E which is an excellent antioxidant. These oils will not break down or become unstable.

Preferred oils for cooking are olive oil (cold pressed, also called extra virgin), sesame oil, rice bran oil, and certain blends. **Blending improves the usage properties of certain oils like shelf life, smoke point, frying stability, taste, and odour.** Some blends in the Indian market use safflower seed (kardi) oil, rice bran oil, soybean oil, and corn oil. For example, using a blend of rice bran and safflower oil, rather than either of them separately, can help reduce cholesterol. Remember, don't let your oil go beyond its smoke point or reuse your oil.

Sesame oil (cold pressed) can be heated to a higher temperature. If you are stir frying, tempering (tarka) your dals, or making stews or curries, use sesame oil. This method of cooking also kills the nutty smell. I figured this out when I was in Orissa conducting many focus study groups on sesame oil. Orissa is the biggest consumer of sesame seed oil in the Indian market.

Good quality olive oil (extra virgin) has a high smoke point, and is perfectly safe to use for frying.

Do not heat your flax seed oil as it destroys the Omega 3. It is best consumed raw in salads and juices, and should be stored in the fridge.

CHIA SEEDS—OUR VERY OWN SUBJA

Chia seeds are low in sodium and cholesterol, and are a superfood or 'living foods' which contain high phytonutrient content and are used for healing and strengthening you. It is said that Aztec and Apache warriors took these seeds with them when they went into combat. They are packed with calcium, phosphorus, manganese, dietary fibre, proteins, complex carbohydrates, essential fats, various vitamins and minerals, and are very high in antioxidants. Chia seeds are another very concentrated source of Omega 3 besides flax seeds, and help in maintaining good digestive health by providing essential fatty acids, which are much needed for the heart. They are also great for maintaining optimum sugar levels and reducing sugar cravings.

How to eat them?

- Soak them in water till they soften or increase in size as they absorb water. Eat as is or add 2 tsp at a time to anything.
- Add them to your protein drinks and juices.
- Add them to oats or any porridge you may have in the mornings.
- Sprinkle on pancakes, dosas, or into your idli batter.
- Mix them in your atta.
- Add them to salads, pasta sauces, or garnish vegetables with them.
- Add to poha, couscous, or millet (see Recipe section).

The good saturated fats

Most of my friends are horrified when I tell them that I use ghee and coconut oil in my food, and are rarely convinced about their good properties. Let's take a minute and educate ourselves on this subject.

There are three types of fatty acid chains—long, medium, and short. Longer-chain fatty acids need to be digested by bile salts (secreted by the gall bladder); short-chain fatty acids are taken in directly during lipid digestion, i.e. when consuming liquid fat (oil). Both short and medium-chain fatty acids are used directly for energy production; medium-chain fatty acids are broken down almost immediately by enzymes in the saliva and gastric juices so that pancreatic fat-digesting enzymes are not even essential. Therefore, there is less strain on the pancreas and digestive system and they are used directly for energy and bypass this process. They do not have any negative effect on people with cholesterol or heart disease. Both coconut oil and ghee have medium chain fatty acids (MCFAs).

MCFAs: THE ENERGY POWERHOUSE

Here's an interesting study. At a race, cyclists who pedalled for three hours were each given a beverage to drink during the last hour. Those who received beverages containing medium-chain fatty acids outperformed the others. Many sports drinks and energy bars sold at health food stores contain MCFAs to provide a quick source of energy.

1) GHEE

Ghee features everywhere in Indian cooking. And there's a good reason for it. According to the Ayurvedic tradition, it enhances 'ojas' (Sanskrit for vigour), an essence that governs the tissues of the body and balances the hormones. Apart from that, ghee has a very high smoke point and doesn't burn easily during cooking. It has more stable saturated bonds and so is less likely to form dangerous free radicals when cooking. During the process of clarifying milk to obtain ghee, proteins are removed and it becomes lactose free, thereby increasing its nutritional value. The fatty acid (butyric acid) that ghee contains has anti-viral properties and is believed to inhibit the growth of cancerous tumours. It also has antioxidant value and aids in the absorption of minerals and vitamins from food.

Okay, so that doesn't mean you start eating it by the spoonfuls. Upto 1 tbs a day is all that's required to keep your skin glowing and to add richness to your food. A word of caution to people with high cholesterol: ghee, at the end of the day, is still saturated fat and needs to be consumed carefully.

2) Coconut Oil

Years of eating foods rich in trans fats, deep fried food, and other harmful fat sources makes it difficult for people to digest fat. And what is the result? It goes into your fat cells. Because coconut oil has MCFAs (lauric acid 50 percent), it does not require bile for digestion. The body turns these fatty acids directly into energy, making it apt for losing weight. In 1998, researchers at McGill University discovered that, compared to other types of fatty acids, MCFAs (in coconut oil) use up energy when processed, and act as weight loss agents. Lauric acid is proven to be antibacterial and antifungal, and it helps keep your immunity strong. Coconut oil is one of the most potent sources of lauric acid, and for this experts say it should be called an 'essential fatty acid'.

Coconut oil took centre stage because of Dr Mary Enig, an international expert on fats, when she first referred to it as the queen of saturated fats because of its special properties. It has a 'thermogenic effect', raising your body temperature and boosting your energy and metabolic rate, which aids weight loss. According to Enig, eliminating fat altogether or intake of low fat foods causes your body to store more fat. Bad carb consumption can cause blood sugar surges and drops. As a result, you lack sustained energy, and experience hunger. Eating the right fats stabilizes blood sugar levels and provides a steady fuel supply throughout the day. When you consume healthy amounts of good quality saturated fats, the body needs less of the Omega 3 and Omega 6 (essential fatty acids). You'll have more energy for work, exercise, and social activities, which will directly lead to a healthy lifestyle. **If you have trouble digesting fats, or are coming out of a low or no fat approach to diet, it's best to start with coconut oil.**

How to use coconut oil to aid weight loss?

- Include coconut in your diet in the following forms: coconut oil, coconut milk, unsweetened desiccated coconut, coconut cream, creamed coconut, coconut water, or in any other form that you can think of.

- Twenty minutes before each meal, take some cold pressed coconut oil as an infusion in warm water or herbal teas (Adding fat to a meal helps lower the glycemic index of the meal. This means that food is absorbed much more slowly into the bloodstream rather than a quick spike in your sugars).

  - If you weigh 40 to 60 kgs, take 1 tbs before each meal, for a total of 3 tbs a day.
  - If you weigh 60 to 80 kgs, take 1½ tbs before each meal, for a total of 4½ tbs a day.
  - If you weigh over 80 kgs, take 2 tbs before each meal, for a total of 6 tbs a day.

- Add coconut milk to curries, stews, vegetable juices, soups, vegetables, salad dressings, cakes (instead of milk), brown rice (pulao), and smoothies.

Note: On any diet you must eat half your fats from the good saturated fats or you will have trouble keeping energy between meals, which will cause carbohydrate cravings. You must get in 2 to 6 grams of Omega 3 and the rest can be Omega 9s (see the Fat table). Also, you can add 1 tsp of cod liver or flax oil before breakfast, if you include Omega 3 in your daily meals.

FATS		
Saturated	**Unsaturated**	
	Monounsaturated Fats (MUFAs)	Polyunsaturated Fats (PUFAs)
• Meats, dairy foods, butter or margarine, hydrogenated oils, coconut oil, ghee.	• Avocado, olive, pumpkin, almond, cashew, sesame, peanut, and rice bran oil.	• Flax, sunflower, corn, soy, walnuts, safflower (kardi), fish oils, salmon.
	• Grains/legumes: buckwheat, chickpeas, millet, miso, quinoa, brown rice, soybean.	Omega 3 is only found in flax and chia seeds (subja).
These fats are stored in tissues, arteries, blood. Contributes to heart attacks, strokes and many other deadly diseases, and makes blood sticky since saturated fats do not assimilate. Except for ghee and coconut oil which are considered the good saturated fats.	• Better for cooking.	Have all the 3 Omegas —3, 6, and 9. Essential fatty acids (EFAs)=10 percent of daily calorie intake.

	• Helps to lose that belly weight, burns fat stores, reduces cholesterol, and risk of strokes. • Helps to normalize sugar levels, lessen food cravings, and reduces inflammation, increases memory, libido, and energy.	Omega 3 reduces inflammation, protects against arthritis, skin conditions, depression, blood and cardiovascular conditions, absorbs fat soluble vitamins, maintains a healthy brain, skin, bones, and teeth, and reduces LDL and cholesterol levels.
		• Omega 6 maintains healthy skin, hair, and nails. • Helps maintain emotional and hormonal balance. • Helps control PMS. • Chia (subja) seeds are mostly used for good bowel movement.
	Tips on how to use fats in your diet: • Sautê in olive oil at a lower temperature. • Make a butter out of plain avocado and have on toast.	• Use flax seed oil in salads, ground to powder, and mix in water, juices, atta for rotis.

	• Make nut butters at home and use as a dip with vegetable sticks like white radish, carrot, and cucumber. • Have ½ cup pumpkin seeds as a snack daily.	• Chia (subja) seeds need to be soaked in water and then consumed after they soften. The black floating stuff in your falooda is this. • Fish oils can be taken as a supplement.

READING THE NUTRITIONAL FACTS OF A BOX OF COOKIES

Food Label	
Cookies	
NUTRITION FACTS	
Serving size 15 Cookies (30g)	
Serving Size Per Container 12	
Amount per serving Calories 140 Calories from fat 40	
	%Daily Value
Total fat 4.5 g	7%
Saturated fat 1 g	5%
Cholesterol 0mg	0%
Sodium 280 mg	12%
Total carbohydrate 20g	7%
Dietary fibre less than 1 g	3%
Sugars less than 1g	
Protein 4 g	
Vitamin A 0% Vitamin C 0%	
Calcium 4% Iron 6%	

Percent Daily Values are based on a 2000 calorie diet.	
Total fat less than 65g	
Saturated fat less than 20g	
Cholesterol less than 300mg	
Sodium less than 2400mg	
Total carbohydrate 300g	
Dietary fibre 25g	

Ingredients: Oat flour, iron, folic acid, enzymes, milk solids, sugar, shortening canola oil, yeast, food grade colours

Interpretation of the above food label	
Serving size 15 cookies (30g)	A quantity (such as 11 chips), weight (28g) or a volume (1 cup).
Serving size per container 12	A quick look at this number will provide an idea of whether the designated serving size is enough to satisfy you. This box contains about 12 servings of cookies. Many people would easily consume a quarter of a box—at least three servings.
Amount per serving	
Calories: 140 Calories from Fat: 40	Number of calories in the listed serving size. In this box, a serving contains 140 calories.
% Daily Value	

Total fat 4.5g 7%	Number of fat grams per serving. Each serving of these cookies has 4.5 grams of fat. Each gram of fat contains 9 calories. If you are attempting to limit fat content to the recommended 15 percent of you daily diet, a single serving of 15 crackers uses up to 13 percent of the entire day's allowance of fat, based on a diet of 2000 calories a day.
Saturated fat 1g 5%	
Cholesterol 0mg 0%	Milligrams per serving.
Sodium 280mg 12%	Milligrams per serving.
Total carbohydrate 20g 7%	The combined total of three types of carbohydrates: dietary fibre, simple sugars, and complex carbohydrates.
Dietary fibre less than 1g 3%	**Fibre:** Grams per serving. The recommended amount of fibre per day is 25 to 35 grams. One serving of these cookies contains less than 1 gram.
Sugars less than 1g	Number of grams of simple sugars per serving. In this example, less than 1 of the 20 grams of carbohydrate come from simple sugars (sucrose, fructose, honey). The idea is to fill your diet with calories that come from complex carbohydrates and protein.

Protein 4g	Grams per serving.
Vitamin A 0% **Vitamin C** 0%	Listed as percentages based on the Recommended Daily Allowances.
Calcium 4% **Iron** 6%	
Percent Daily Values are based on a 2000 calorie diet.	This column lists percentages based on the Agriculture Department's recommended diet of 30 percent of calories from fat. The guidelines envision a diet of 2000 calories a day, with no more than 600 from fat.
Total fat less than 65g	**Calories from fat:** Of the number of calories in the serving, how many come from fat. If you are trying to limit your fat intake to no more than 15 percent of your daily calories, you would have to balance higher-fat foods like this with foods that have nearly no fat.
Saturated fat less than 20g	Of the total fat grams, this is the amount of saturated fat, a category that is listed separately because saturated fats are thought to increase the risk of heart disease. This listing does not include trans-hydrogenated fatty acids, which are polyunsaturated fats that have been chemically altered to have a longer shelf life. These trans-hydrogenated fats have been shown to increase cholesterol

	levels. These fats can be identified in the ingredient section of the food label as 'partially hydrogenated oil'.
Cholesterol less than 300mg	
Sodium less than 2400mg	
Total carbohydrate 300g	
Dietary fibre 25g	
Ingredients: Oat flour, iron, folic acid, enzymes, milk solids, sugar, shortening (partially hydrogenated) canola oil, yeast, food grade colours	

6 WAYS TO BALANCE AND PURGE FAT:

1. Fried foods are better absorbed when eaten with grated white radish (mooli) as the very action of mooli is to dissolve fats effectively (see p 104). Now I know you can't carry this around, but you can ask for it at a restaurant. Vegetables which help to dissolve fats are white radish (mooli), red radish, onions, leekh, and turnip.

2. A little extra salty food will balance out the oils consumed. So the day your food is greasy, add more salt (of course rock or sea salt). Similarly, too much salt in your diet will make you crave bad quality fats in the form of deep-fried food. So watch out for too much salt.

3. Minimize the intake of animal food which includes dairy, refined and hydrogenated oils, all foods that

are fried or come out of a packet (even though they say fat free), simple sweeteners such as sugar, cane sugar, all other sugars, and sugar derivatives.

4. When frying, use the oil-water sauté method (that is, use half of each to start a sauté).

5. Choose cold pressed, unrefined oils, and supplement diet with nuts, seeds, and fish oils [if non vegetarian] (flax, chia, sunflower, pumpkin, and cod liver).

6. Avoid polyunsaturated oils such as corn sunflower, soy, or safflower (alone), unless blended, for cooking. Use monosaturated oils like flax, chia seed, and pumpkin seed oils for salads and dressings.

WHILE ON A WEIGHT-LOSS PLAN:

- It's best to limit oil to 1 tbs a day. Get the rest of your fat from food sources, unless using the coconut oil weight loss initiative I have suggested.
- Cut back on red meat consumption and fatty fish such as salmon and trout, which is otherwise good for you.
- Nuts (and nut butters) are high in fat, so even though you do need them, cut them out while on a weight-loss plan.
- Avoid all trans fats and saturated fats (barring coconut oil and ghee), so basically all processed and packaged products.
- Dairy should be definitely minimized. So butter, margarine, paneer, yoghurt, cheese, and milk solids are out.
- Animal foods should also be minimized.

- Get the good fats from flax, avocados, pumpkin, sunflower, and chia seeds.
- Read food labels carefully.

4) Animal Protein

Protein has two main functions: one is to boost growth and repair body tissues (including skin, hair, and nails), and the other is for the production of hormones, neuro-transmitters, antibodies, and energy. Protein builds cells, tissues, enzymes, and helps to digest our food. Our brain chemicals need protein to help manufacture all the brain chemicals. People who lack protein in their diet usually make up for it up by eating sugar and having coffee—as this stimulates their brain chemistry for a short period of time.

When we think of protein, we automatically think of animal sources of protein. I'm often asked: where is the protein in a vegetarian-based diet? (see p 81 on where to get vegetable sources of protein). Many of my clients balk at the idea of leaving their much loved poultry because they are constantly told by their fitness instructors, that they need to be on a meat-based (non vegetarian) diet to build up muscle mass. And if they stay off the red meat, they're healthy. As explained in Chapter 2, all animal food is yang. If you eat foods from the extreme yang energy polarity, you will be creating health issues for yourself. Excess yang produces strong contracted energy in the body which then needs to be discharged. Anything yang also desires yin, so a meat eater will either eat a lot of sugar (yin), alcohol (yin), or drink a lot of water (yin) to compensate for this yang. Another reason why too much meat is not recommended because it leads to the build up of a large load of uric acid, making the kidneys work harder to get rid of it from the body. So the solution to this issue is simple, eat moderate amounts of animal protein (approximately under 120 grams if eaten daily), and balance it with good quality carbohydrates like whole grains, legumes/beans, and vegetables.

6 REASONS WHY YOU SHOULD MINIMIZE ANIMAL PROTEIN:

1. Animal protein increases the acidic level in blood, as it takes longer to digest, thus creating an overload in the body.
2. Besides being high on fats, it causes a build up of amino acids which have not been used during digestion, to get stored as fat.
3. The structure, density of meat and all animal food, and its contractedness hinders free flow of energy available for many activities as it takes a longer time to digest. This slows your energy down.
4. The digestion of meat and all animal food expands and contracts your intestines, so all your organ functions go into a maximum load position. This essentially means that animal food takes a longer time to digest. Therefore you end up producing a lot of heat—within the body and externally. As the body is in push mode, you get easily aggravated and also lethargic. This also leads to aggressive behavioural patterns.
5. The digestion of meats results in the production of certain acids which must be counteracted by the use

of calcium stores in your body. So it will actually end up depleting calcium.

6. Sulphur, which is present in meat, limits the calcium assimilation process in the body.

All those meat eaters who just can't give up on meat should switch to fish instead. It's healthier and rich in amino acids, vitamins, minerals, and essential fatty acids while being lower in saturated fat than meat. Fish is also high in Vitamin B12 and Vitamin D. If you eat one serving, half of your protein requirements for the day are taken care of. And if you just can't give it up, then try to have salads (raw/cooked) and good quality desserts—those made with natural sweeteners and not sugar—with your non-vegetarian food (see Recipe section).

BALANCING ANIMAL FOOD PROTEIN

Have you ever been to a gym for three to four months, reduced your carbs, eaten your protein, generally been good, and stepped onto the scales on the fifth month to find that you haven't really lost much weight? This is probably because you have consumed too much meat in the period and neglected your essential carbs. After the protein quota is used up in the body (that which is digestible), the balance goes into toxic build up of mucous, which makes you sluggish. This then attracts you to sugar, alcohol, or coffee, all yin, making your weight-loss plan go haywire. You need to learn how to balance the protein you get from animal foods and know how to eat them.

To reduce the risk of what animal protein can do to you, you should be eating a little under $^1/_3$ kg of meat daily. By meat I mean red meat, chicken, beef, and also cheese.

On the other hand, vegetarian sources of protein (see list below), which are concentrated in protein, can be consumed safely up to double the amount of animal protein foods.

GOOD SOURCES OF VEGETABLE PROTEIN:

1 **All legumes and beans**: This includes tofu which is fermented soybean. Do not be swayed by protein powders, as they are too concentrated and do not assimilate and digest easily.

2 **Grain**: All grains, particularly amaranth (rajgeera) and quinoa, which are higher in their protein content than the others.

3 All **green and yellow vegetables** help the synthesis of protein in the liver, which is very important, especially for weight loss.

4 **Good quality fermented foods**: These are easily digested as they have been broken down already by good bacteria, and are also rich in protein.

5 **Nuts and seeds**: Concentrated forms of both protein and fat. These include flax, pumpkin, sunflower, walnuts, and almonds.

6 **Spirulina**: This is rich in trace minerals, chlorophyll, and is the highest source of concentrated protein you will find (in Western markets you will find a larger range).

EGGS

Eggs, again, are yang and contracted in nature. An egg contains 50 percent water, 34 percent fats, and 16 percent protein, and the yolk contains more than two thirds of your daily dose of recommended cholesterol. They supply the body with a concentrated source of energy and can be beneficial for those who feel weak. Because they are the most concentrated version of an animal food, if consumed in excess, they will cause a drying effect in the body and make you crave for sweets, spicy foods, sodas, and colas as these foods temporarily balance out its extreme yang nature. That's why you see most people who eat eggs, add spicy sauces, green onions, and other foods that will help balance and digest the concentrated nature of eggs. The fats (34 percent) in the eggs, if consumed in excess, do not digest, but cause deposits in your body (especially in women's reproductive areas with mucous), adversely affect the thyroid gland, and cause digestive problems.

B12 AND THE VEGETARIAN

Your body needs thirteen types of vitamins (some of which are not produced in the body) which build tissue, keeps your organs strong, immunity, help absorb food, flush out toxins, keep your cellular structure strong, and more. You need to make sure you are getting all the necessary vitamins from your diet. The B group of vitamins is essential and needs to be included in your daily diet, either through food or from supplements. Out of the 13, Vitamin B12 is the most important vitamin. A slight deficiency of Vitamin B12 can lead to anaemia, fatigue, mania, and depression, while a long term deficiency can potentially cause permanent damage to the brain and central nervous system. It supports metabolic processes involving the digestive, circulatory, and respiratory systems. It also aids in red blood cell formation and helps to maintain the neurological processes of the central nervous system. Although Vitamin B12 is primarily found in animal protein, the following foods are also rich in it:

- All beans from whole to split beans (dals) when sprouted
- Spirulina
- Fermented foods such as tofu (from soybean), miso (available in Indian markets today), quick pickles (see Sauerkraut recipe p 280) made at home, yoghurt made with almond milk and seed milk

Things that deplete B12: Excessive sugar, intoxicants including marijuana, drugs, and alcohol, antibiotics, a dysfunctional liver, birth control pills. Stress and prolonged illness is also a major contributor.

5) A pinch of salt

Take a look at your plate of food. There's your bowl of rice, vegetables, dal, a roti or two, some freshly cut salad, and...wait...what's that tiny little heap of salt sitting beside those cucumbers? This is what a regular Indian plate full of food looks likes. Let's face it, we Indians love our salt. So much so that most of the times our food tastes only of salt, because we use so much of it. It ends up masking the actual taste of vegetables, lentils, and anything else we might be eating. Just because we fought for it, doesn't mean we need to smother our food in it.

Most people usually take in at least one extra tsp of salt every day. This is in addition to the processed foods they eat on an almost daily basis, which also have a very high salt content. While we do need sodium for our cells to function and to manage the nutrients in our body, excessive sodium can be detrimental for us. Sodium acts like a pump (flushing out excess toxins from our cells and bringing in the nutrients to them) and high levels of sodium in your diet not only cause water retention adding weight, but also lead to high blood pressure (as blood pressure is regulated by sodium in the body). Adults need less than 2400 milligrams of sodium, which is 1 tsp of table salt (of which 40 percent is sodium).

Common table salt (or refined salt as we know it) contains high quantities of chemicals with 99.5 percent of it constituting sodium chloride, dextrose (sugar), potassium iodide, and much more. This salt has been stripped off its mineral content and adds nothing in terms of nutritional value, except taste. It makes the blood acidic, and weakens digestion. People who have a high intake of sodium have a high incidence of hypertension and stroke.

FOODS WITH HIGH SODIUM LEVELS

• Various dairy products such as cheese, butter, eggs, whipped toppings, ice cream, and flavoured yoghurt

- Condiments such as soy sauce, and other bottled sources not made fresh
- All processed meats (salami, ham, bacon, sausages, etc.)
- Canned foods such as soups, vegetables, and refined foods
- Bread, tomato sauce, cakes, and biscuits

THE RIGHT SALTS

We cannot escape the fact that we need salt in our daily food. That is why it is imperative to eat the right salt. Rock salt or sea salt is a better option than regular table salt as they are almost entirely sodium chloride, with only traces of other elements (minerals) because both retain their minerals, especially sea salt. Regular salt has been stripped off all its essential minerals. Rock or sea salt, being alkaline, also helps to neutralize the effects of acid-forming foods. For example, grain is from the acid food group (we need both acid and alkaline foods), and if we add a pinch of sea salt, it neutralizes this acid content. This is one reason why people salt their meats, since meat will cause an acidic blood condition. Good quality salt will strengthen your digestion and will help in bowel movement while bad quality salt will do just the opposite. If you are trying to maintain stable sugar levels, watch your weight, and keep your cravings down, the right salt is an important factor. The nature of salt is to add an earthy flavour to food, and give your body the same earthiness.

The job of the kidneys is to regulate body fluids by eliminating toxins from the body. The proper elimination of toxins is imperative to keep normal body weight. Water retention for example is a sign that the kidneys are not working properly. The consumption of the right salt (which is the flavor attached to the kidneys in the Traditional Chinese Medicine system) thus becomes crucial and a regulating factor for this metabolic process of the kidneys.

HOW TO USE SALT

To maintain the acid/alkaline balance, the sodium/potassium (also present in body cells) balance in the body must be maintained too. An increase in potassium intake offsets the adverse effect that sodium has on blood pressure. Potassium is found in fruits and vegetables (especially spinach and parsley).

- Eat vegetables lightly cooked, as opposed to overcooked. When spinach is overcooked, it loses up to 50 percent of its potassium.
- Balance salt cravings with the right yin food; include honey (potassium), sweet vegetables (see home remedy section), fruits like cantaloupe, dates, kiwi, dry figs, oranges, and pears. By eating whole natural foods prescribed in this approach, you can keep the sodium/potassium balance you require.
- Salt dominates the other flavours of your meal. Use it only to flavour your food. Recipe books advise you to add 'salt to taste' for a good reason.
- Switch to sea salt or rock salt.
- Try sesame salt or gomasio sesame salt (see recipe on p 316) if you crave too much salt. The combination of oil and minerals from the salt helps your blood

condition to stay more alkaline and also gives you the calcium that you require.

The transition to every new diet should always be gradual, for your body needs to understand the changes that it will go through. You need to ease your body into it. Don't suddenly quit having meat or eggs one day if you've been eating them all your life. Let it go gradually. For tomorrow is always another day. Give up one thing at a time, such as red meat first, then poultry. This way you won't shock your body, or deprive it of what it craves. I'm never too hard on my clients if they slip. Also be aware that you may go through what I call a 'discharge', which could range from headaches, to body pain, cold, flu, body odour, mucous, a digestive imbalance (colitis or constipation), need to sleep or insomnia, boils, pimples, etc. But these are all temporary, as your body is adjusting to new wholesome foods. Nevertheless, here are some tips on how the transition can be made easy.

Tips for Transitioning into The Beauty Diet:

1. If you eat white rice, change to brown rice.
2. If you eat commercial white bread daily, minimize that and change to roti instead—if you are gluten intolerant, use a different flour such as sorghum (jovar), rajgeera (amaranth), foxtail millet (cheena), buckwheat (kuttu); these are gluten free.
3. If you eat salad—make your own dressing, instead of using commercial bottled readymade dressing; and cook (boil, blanch, sauté) your salad more often than eating it raw.

4. If you have chocolate every day, you may consider replacing it with 70 percent dark chocolate for starters, and then graduate to a darker version.

5. If you have eggs and toast for breakfast every day, do it thrice a week, and replace it with a cooked porridge or grain breakfast on the balance days (see grain recipes), this goes for breakfast cereals out of a box as well. Replace milk with almond milk (see recipe on p 256) or water for porridge.

6. If you snack on junk in between, replace with homemade snacks or minimize junk snacks and increase homemade snacks.

7. If you drink a lot of black Indian tea, or coffee, then intersperse it with green or herbal teas or get the sugar out of there for starters.

8. If you have a lot of sugar in your tea and coffee, replace it with stevia—this goes for sweets too.

9. Grab a fruit in between meals during a lean period, that is when your stomach has digested your meal; usually 1 to 2 hours.

10. Make sure you always start one meal in the day with a soup (we will understand how this works in the soup section).

11. If you use table salt, replace it with rock or sea salt.

12. If you use refined oil, replace it with cold pressed sesame, olive, rice bran, or blended oils.

13. If you use dairy products, find substitutes such as silken tofu or regular tofu to cream dishes and nut milk instead of milk.

14. If you don't do seeds at all—please start adding them to your daily meals; minimize nuts on a weight-loss plan.

5

WHAT TO EAT

You've had a whole chapter of 'what not to eat'. But now we move on to the real deal, 'the what to eat' list. Because this is the part that will change your life, and set you on that path to beauty. The key mantra here is **grains, beans, greens, fruit, fish,** and **fermented foods**—the building blocks of a new you. Keep that in mind and you'll never go wrong. But first, let me tell you how I got Neha Dhupia to lose her weight, but more importantly to regain her health.

Neha Dhupia and the Beauty Diet

I'll never forget what Neha said to me the first time we met. 'I eat everything, so please don't keep me off carbs in the evening. I trust you know what you are doing, and I'll go with it.' It's rare to have someone trust you so implicitly, and she did. Her goal was to lose weight but be healthy.

As a counsellor and a health chef, I tend to be like a horse with blinkers on, concentrating only on the proper assimilation of foods in the body, so that 100 percent of its nutrients are utilized. When you do that, there is no chance of any extras which will add to the fat. If you go back to what I said in the previous chapter, you'll know that fats that come from animal foods and dairy will settle on a woman's fat-prone areas, typically her thighs and hips. By using a combination of good quality, nutritionally efficient foods, the Beauty Diet seeks to purge this fat and balance you out. The benefit of this approach is that the unnecessary weight you're holding on to will automatically begin to shed, even if it is in the so called problem areas.

I followed the same format of cooking for Neha—lots of greens every day, whole grains (initially for six months in both meals, then at lunch only), beans and fish (dinners thrice a week), vegetables, lots of good quality fermented foods, and soup with miso daily. I used different cooking techniques in balance, so she got a lot of energy for her shoots, and food that kept her interested and excited.

I soon noticed that she had started losing weight, and told her about it. Her reaction to this was, 'People say I have lost weight, I tell the whole world about you.' Of course she trains a lot, so that added an additional benefit to the whole process. What was more of a victory for me was not her weight loss but the fact that she wanted to know everything about this approach to eating. So I educated her, we talked, and she mentioned that sometimes her blood counts would not be within normal range; like the ones related to the hormones. I knew this had some connection to weight gain, something she was not really worried about, but it did come up. I assured her that with this kind of an approach, she should not be concerned about her counts. This is the most balanced approach to keeping your body functions in balance. Sometime back she mentioned she wanted to get her blood tests done and I said it was a good idea. I woke up the next morning to find a bbm from her saying 'Shonali, I can't thank you enough. My reports are absolutely normal and it's all thanks to your food!' This is what she had to say after being on this approach for over two years now:

I have learnt how to eat well and have gradually become accustomed to this approach. Shonali teaches you the 'middle path' so that I could be travelling anywhere, but my eating remains within the parameters she has given me. My blood counts have been corrected and I feel they had an association to fat in the body. The diet is cleansing you daily, so it shows on your skin, hair, also in your mind and attitude. My body feels extremely balanced mentally and physically. You will only know the wonders this approach works on you when you actually try it!

NEHA DHUPIA—ACTOR

So here are the basic dietary musts that you should never ignore. And there's no picking and choosing among them. No 'I hate veggies' or 'Whoa! I don't eat carbs'. To be beautiful, you have to give your body the best that nature has to offer.

THE WHAT-TO-EAT KEY:

1) Grains
2) Greens and veggies
3) Beans
4) Fish (if non vegetarian)
5) Fruit
6) Good quality fermented foods

The essential top three being **grains**, **greens**, and **beans**.

1) Go Grains: Say yes to carbs. The right kind, that is.

When I started my work in India with advocating whole grains, I realized I was up against a big myth that floated around among people on a weight-loss programme. The no carb diet. Myth. Myth. Myth! A no-carb diet denies you of the very fuel you need to not only lose weight, but also to keep your digestive system functioning like a well-oiled machine. Do that and you'll be left tired and cranky at the end of the day. We need complex carbohydrates to function when moving onto a healthier platform of health, and that's the simple truth.

Instead of a no-carb diet, increase the complex carbs in your diet; and you are on your way to weight loss. It also keeps you fuller for a longer period, as sugars are broken down slowly, and they don't get absorbed by your fat cells. We all need these carbohydrates as they are one of the macronutrients, the other two being fat and protein.

For centuries, whole or cereal grain has been the most important source of nutrition for human beings. They are self preserving and are rich in minerals, fibre, vitamins, and phytochemicals, which strengthen the spleen, pancreas, and soothe the stomach. Whole grains have fibre of the insoluble variety, and they actually prevent weight gain, cancers, and other ailments. They are the most complete food you can eat. Whole cereal grains make us whole, just like they are complete in themselves. **If you cut complex carbohydrates, you will crave more of the sugary stuff. And if you survive only on raw salads and juices, it will leave you hungry.** So to cut cravings and lose weight, eat your whole grains (preferably 'unprocessed').

Note: Be careful of consuming too much whole grain (especially brown rice) if you have irritable bowel syndrome (IBS) or disorder (IBD). Too much fibre can irritate the stomach. However, if you suffer from these conditions, eating whole grain in moderation is beneficial as these fibres bulk up our stools and keep the digestive system healthy.

Gain from grain for your brain

In stressful times like ours, we need to keep our brain happy and at peace. The food we eat plays a large role in this. Do you know why yoga advocates a sattvic diet of eating fresh vegetables and fruit instead of meat and other foods which increase heat and inactivity in the body? It's not because of cultural or traditional reasons. It's because vegetables and whole grains are the first source of energy. The brain's main source of energy is glucose; however, the need for glucose doesn't mean that loading up on soft drinks, desserts, and sweets is going to make it any smarter.

Whole grains break down the complex carbohydrates, which creates a peaceful rise in blood sugars and the production of neurotransmitters—chemicals that facilitate communication among brain cells or neurons. For example, the neurotransmitter serotonin regulates sleep and pain and influences moods. When serotonin is in low supply, it manifests itself in the form of insomnia and a depressed mood.

Whole grains give you what you need when it comes to a complete nutritional profile from food. But let's look at brown rice around which all else is built in this diet.

5 reasons why you should switch to earthy brown rice

In India, we are rediscovering brown rice (see Recipe section), and I would like to see it as a staple just as wheat (*gehu*) features on our dining tables. Food has its own energies, and if you go back to the yin and yang chart, grain is yang and among this brown rice has strong yang energy as opposed to yin, dispersing energy. Treat it like a daily elixir for your system. Jessica Porter, author of *The Hip Chick's Guide to Macrobiotics,* says, 'Brown rice strikes a balance between minerals, protein, and carbohydrates in such a way that it mirror's natures energies beautifully.'

1) Brown rice impacts blood sugar levels positively. A complex carbohydrate, when chewed properly, gives you a steady supply of the right sugars, which will keep you energetic throughout the day.

2) It has about seventy anti-ageing antioxidants, especially Vitamin E, which we all know is super good for a beautiful you.
3) Brown rice is abundant with B vitamins and trace minerals, the only thing that works for that perfect glow on your face, abundant and shiny hair, and nails (something that an Indian diet lacks).

THE SUPER GRAINS: AMARANTH AND QUINOA

Amaranth, or rajgeera in Hindi, is a whole grain (also used as flour) that has higher calcium and protein levels than milk. When combined with other grains, it's amino-acid profiles are higher than meat. If you can sprout these grains, it is an invaluable pellet of energy and nutrition. It is excellent for people who want a rich source of protein or are trying to lose weight, and for nursing women, as well as children, especially if your child is lactose intolerant. Also, if you are in a transition from non vegetarian to vegetarian food, and your body is still getting used to protein from vegetarian sources, consider combining amaranth with another grain (like wheat or sorghum [jovar]), and use a couple of times a week to keep up the protein factor in your body. It is rich in Vitamin C which combats coughs, colds, and flus. I use amaranth flour in a roti and combine it with spinach or fenugreek. The texture is amazing and whenever I have guests, they have complimented me on how good they feel eating it. I also make amaranth muffins combined with sorghum flour; it makes them gluten free and a good protein snack.

Quinoa (pronounced keen-vah) is an amino acid (protein) and magnesium-rich seed. Native to South America, quinoa was once called 'the gold of the Incas', who recognized its value in increasing the stamina of their warriors. This grain relaxes your blood vessels resulting in fewer headaches (great for people with migraine) and also decreases the incidence of hypertension and strokes. It is also gluten free and easy to digest. Quinoa can be had in a poha or as a morning porridge combined with nuts and nut milks.

4) It is also rich in antioxidants like Q10 (produced in the body), which facilitates the transformation of fats and sugars into energy, reducing obesity, counteracting ageing, and also great for diabetics. Brown rice will actually help burn fat due to the presence of gamma oryzanol, another antioxidant, which converts fat to lean body mass. Brown rice has an enzyme antioxidant that will reduce mucous in your body and boost the lungs. It also contains alpha lipoic acid, another antioxidant that helps the liver rejuvenate and slows down the ageing process.

5) Rice bran, when fermented, boosts your internal organs, especially the thymus, adrenals, and thyroid. When my father had cancer, we gave him a rice bran and shiitake mushroom extract (MGN-3) which stimulates the natural killer cells and boosts immunity. His doctors were always surprised that his blood counts and vital parameters stayed normal, and asked me what I was giving him. Brown rice will help support your immune function.

#See Recipe section for delicious brown rice recipes

KNOW YOUR GLUTEN

WHAT IS GLUTEN INTOLERANCE?

If a person is gluten intolerant, it means he or she will react almost instantaneously to wheat and other products such as oats, pastas, maida, processed flours, and barley flour, all of which have gluten. Symptoms could range from bloating, burping, wheezing, gas, irritable bowel syndrome, fatigue, and mood fluctuations. Some people live with gluten intolerance for years without detecting the problem. To top it all, no doctor can diagnose you immediately; allergy tests are recommended if you can't zero in on the likely cause of the symptoms.

You should eliminate processed foods made with white flour and other gluten flours (mentioned above) like pasta (refined flour), cakes, pizzas, white bread, pies, cookies, wheat, most readymade salad dressings, soy sauce, and other sauces.

HOW WILL YOU KNOW IF YOU ARE GLUTEN INTOLERANT?

Keeping a food diary and seeing your reactions to foods having gluten is helpful. Another method would be to eliminate gluten from your diet and see the effects. Also, check all food labels, as gluten appears as starch, emulsifiers, flavourings, hydrogenated plant protein, or stabilizers on most packaged products like baked beans, baking powder, beer, canned meats, and other canned foods, salad dressings, sauces, and cheese products. Fortunately, anyone with gluten intolerance has enough options. These are sorghum (jovar), amaranth, known as rajgeera in most shops; buckwheat, known as (kuttu) or soba noodles in speciality stores; cornmeal—makai ka atta in regular grocery stores or polenta in speciality stores; brown rice flour—which can even be made at home by grinding brown rice as you do wheat flour and quinoa available in specialty stores only. These could be used in place of any gluten grain in your diet.

Shekhar Kapur joined my programme because he was gluten intolerant, and I understood how to work with his needs. It is easy for Shekhar to maintain a gluten-free approach abroad, but while he is here he takes his meals from me. Here's what he has to say after starting on the gluten free diet:

'Shonali's approach to food was just what the doctor never ordered. I did not realize that a diet could so fundamentally alter even the way I think. I wish I had known all this earlier. Before I would wonder why I was constantly fatigued, but that stopped when I found Shonali's gluten-free diet. And I didn't ever need to compromise the Punjabi in me. She would even rustle up delicious rajma chawal whenever I felt like eating some comfort food.' SHEKHAR KAPUR—FILM DIRECTOR

How do you know if you are eating whole grains

Any food with a modicum of whole grain in it can be labelled 'whole grain'. If it says 'enriched' or 'stone ground' in the first ingredient, put it right back on the shelf. **What you should be looking out for is the word 'whole' in the first ingredient.** In India, unfortunately, the food laws are not so strict to have all ingredients mentioned on the package. And even bread which claims to be 'wheat bran' or 'whole grain' will have some amount of processed white flour in it. A good serving of whole grain will have 3 grams of fibre or more per serving.

Diabetics have this notion that all rice is bad for them. This is absolutely false. It is perfectly safe for diabetics to consume brown rice and any other whole grain. Please refer to the whole grain list. See recommended shopping list on grains (p 139).

2) Gorgeous Greens

Hate it or love it, we have to come to terms with the fact that there's nothing better for our bodies than our veggies. They contain protein, carbohydrates, fibre, minerals, vitamins, phytochemicals (antioxidants), and other necessary components to sustain us. Eaten with grain, they bring in a balance and have a curative character. The enzymes that veggies contain help to cleanse the digestive system and are especially beneficial for non vegetarians because of the combination of non-vegetarian foods which is yang balanced by the yin of greens. They should constitute 25 to 30 percent of your daily consumption volume.

Each vegetable has its own special quality and you should keep in mind a few factors while picking up what you're about to eat. I'll break them down for you.

(1) Vegetables that grow above the ground have an upward energy. These affect the upper parts of the body, especially the lungs, throat, and heart, and they bring in a lightness and freshness as they bring in oxygen, feeding your cellular structure to produce haemoglobin. All green plants have a substance in them that makes them green namely Chlorophyll. All chlorophyll (green) plants have certain pigments known as carotenes. Chlorophyll and

carotene work together to purify and build blood, renew tissue, promote a healthy intestinal condition, improve liver function, activate enzymes, specially the ones that produce E, A, and K which are all needed to keep you looking good. As these vegetables contain chlorophyll, they improve blood condition and alleviate anaemia.

Examples: Green leafy vegetables such as green onions, spinach, fenugreek (methi), broccoli, parsley, coriander, endive, and Chinese cabbage

(2) Vegetables that grow horizontally have a horizontal spreading energy. These will affect the lower parts and upper part of the body, stomach, colon, and reproductive areas.

Examples: Tubers such as cucumber, zucchini, lotus root (kamal kakdi), and potatoes

(3) Vegetables that push themselves into the ground but have leafs growing above the soil have downward energy. They impart energy to your digestive system, and bring about stability, energy, and confidence.

Examples: Root vegetables such as carrots, white and red radish (mooli), turnips, and beetroots

(4) Vegetables that grow near the surface of the soil have an inward energy. These are similar to root vegetables. Their swollen and round nature helps to bring about a balance in the lower organs, especially when cooked. They also create a warm contracted inward energy in the stomach (see Recipe section on round vegetable soup).

Examples: Round vegetables such as onions, pumpkins, cabbage, cauliflower, and red pumpkin

What does this mean for you?

As a counsellor, I use vegetables to heal people by looking at their properties. For example, a home remedy for bronchial or lung issues is the lotus root drink. Let's see how this works. The lotus root grows in water, and goes down quite deep. It has horizontal or a spreading energy and when cut open, it looks like the insides of your lung chamber with a web-like structure similar to the lung alveoli (lung sacs) and bronchioles. This vegetable, because of all the above mentioned elements, has the capacity to go deep into the lungs, clean them up (of mucous), and restore balance in them. You will only know its healing powers once you take it. This is all due to how it grows, where it grows, and the energy it carries due to these components. Of course this does not mean you go crazy over it.

What we need to do is use the right vegetables, grain, and beans blended with the right cooking styles to achieve balance. For example, radish (mooli) grows through mud, while lotus root (kamal kakdi) grows in the water—and both will have a different energetic influence when you eat them. The radish will be more forceful energy while the lotus root softer, flowing energy. The energetic contribution to your health will also become clearer when I present to you how we use these vegetables in home remedies. The examples mentioned below will clarify my point further.

SCENARIO 1: It's a cold day and you are getting the chills. Plus you've had a harrowing day at work. What would be the right energetic balance for a meal that would be both satisfying and nourishing?

The goal here would be to settle your energy and provide you some warmth.

So given that it's cool outside, yin, we are looking for yang foods and yang cooking styles to give you the warmth. I would recommend a slow cooked (yang) vegetable stew, mainly made of round vegetables like sweet potato, turnips, squash (all yang), and a hearty bean soup with some brown rice thrown in—this will not only nourish you, but will also settle your energies and give your system the warmth it needs. The slow cooking style will provide inward moving energy in the stomach/spleen along with the vegetables used.

SCENARIO 2: If on the other hand it's a hot day, and you have been out baking in the sun (yang energy) and you need to disperse it, what would you do? Could you use the above meal? No, it would make you warmer.

The goal here would be to disperse some of that yang energy to cool you down.

You would perhaps have a half-raw and half-blanched salad (yin) with green onions, asparagus, leafy greens, a cool cucumber soup, and perhaps a light grain like millet to bring about the balance desired. Here the millet is yin compared to brown rice (yang).

#See Recipe section for delicious vegetable recipes.

Wonder vegetables that control cravings and stabilize weight

1) **Sweet vegetables:** Sweet vegetables such as red pumpkin (bhopla), cabbage, carrot, onion, sweet potato, and beetroot are good quality yin foods which will decrease your cravings for sugary food. Although they will take time to show their effects, you will notice the change. The sweetness in these vegetables strengthens your spleen, pancreas, and stomach—the three main organs for digestion and regulation of blood sugar levels.

In weight-loss plans, the first thing that dietitians will tell you is to keep off sweets. What they don't to tell you is that you don't have to deny yourself the sweet flavour which comes from whole natural foods. When you are overpowered with the temptations posed by a chocolate cake, you are less likely to be satisfied with a bowl of sweet boiled vegetables. But if you eat these sweet vegetables regularly, the grip of that chocolate cake will slowly loosen and you will be able to resist it. Sugar from whole grains and vegetables are the necessary ammunition for your muscles, nerves, and a source of energy for all other body functions. You stop craving sweets, as your body is being nurtured by the right sweet flavor all the time. Once your blood sugars are steady, you get stable.

2) **Greens:** Want to lose weight? Then this is one vegetable group you must include in your diet every day. And I mean every single day. The liver is your body's strongest organ and processes fat, protein, and carbohydrates. It also gets rid of bad blood and fluids. Loading your liver with junk, greasy, and processed food will not help you lose weight. All chlorophyll plants help convert carotene to Vitamin A which is present in greens and spirulina. This is essential for correct metabolization of protein in the

body. Greens cleanse your liver and lighten the load. Your liver loves the bitter flavour. Bitter greens (rich in Provitamin A) such as fenugreek (methi), lettuce (arugula), mustard greens (sarson), and asparagus are the best. They will help the liver to breakdown fat and protein, making your liver loaded with bad quality blood. Using lime and bitter flavour with the greens will help rebalance your liver.

3) **Herbs:** The liver loves the pungent flavour of herbs such as bay leaf (tej patta), turmeric (haldi), basil, cardamom (elaichi), cumin (jeera), dill (suha), ginger, black pepper, and mint (pudina). These also keep your weight in check.

4) **Vegetables that melt away your fat and cholesterol and clean your liver:** The fat and protein which you consume is never processed well by the body (if of bad quality); therefore you pack in the weight. White and red radish has everything to aid weight loss (see recipe on p 308 as well for the carrot–white radish remedy). White radish contains all the vitamins and minerals you need to lose weight. It stimulates your thyroid, blood sugar levels, mobilizes sugar, and use of glucose for energy. That does not mean you eat copious amounts of it. Start by including a little bit of it in your diet. Use it in soups (which is the most efficient way for the body to use it) as a side condiment, or cook it as a vegetable. Include turnips, onions, green onions, and leeks as well. Yellow vegetables (carrots, pumpkin [peela kaddu], and sweet potatoes) are rich in Provitamin A, which help to clean your liver.

Spirulina: Hippocrates said, 'Use nature as your physician'. That's why dogs eat leaves, which are full of chlorophyll, to clean out their system. Spirulina is the only sea algae we get in India (available in powder and capsule formats) at the moment and will help to cleanse the liver, as it is a chlorophyll-rich food. Spirulina is rich in chlorophyll, and the properties of foods rich in chlorophyll is to improve liver function by cleansing toxins from the liver. Chlorophyll has a similar molecular structure like haemoglobin (red blood cells), therefore it actually enriches blood. The foods that negatively impact the liver are rich, greasy foods and an excess of animal foods. These foods keep the liver sluggish and this is a major factor for weight gain. The liver stores and purifies blood, allowing more blood for circulation throughout the body. Chlorophyll-rich foods like spirulina aid this circulation. If the liver is stagnant due to being overburdened with the wrong foods, it leads to impure blood causing skin disorders, acne, acidosis, and toxic blood which produces more health issues.

A note on spirulina: You can take 1 heaped tsp or 5 grams of tablets, twice a day, if in good health condition. Some people do not like the flavour, so you may want to disguise this in a vegetable juice (like carrot). Start with ¼ tsp initially if you are just starting it and an hour and a half before meals. A headache or mild indigestion is normal, as it indicates that the algae is working on your system. 1 tsp of spirulina is equal to 1 ounce of beef.

6) **Shiitake mushrooms:** This magical fungus cleans the blood, boosts immunity, helps keep your weight down, and lowers your cholesterol and blood pressure. It impacts your blood condition and regulates your blood sugar levels. Include them in your diet if possible, but please don't overdo it.

#Tip: You need to soak them for about 20 minutes before using them.

7) **The cabbage family:** Broccoli, green and red cabbage, pak choi, cauliflower, turnips (shalgam with greens), knoll khol (ganth gobi) all prevent cancers. When these vegetables are chewed, they release compounds that activate detox-ifying enzymes in the liver, helping the liver to function better. They are also low in fat and will help keep your weight under check.

TIPS ON HOW TO COOK VEGETABLES

1. Cook veggies in minimal water. Let them cook in their own juices. This will help retain their nutrients.

2. Cook them as quickly as possible in the summer and use longer cooking methods in winter or the monsoons. Cover to retain nutrients and preserve flavours.

3. Adding salt earlier in the stages of cooking helps them retain colour. Do not use baking soda or colours to bring out the colour of vegetable, as these are harmful.

4. Cook in stainless steel, cast iron or nonstick coated utensils, as most vegetables contain acid and aluminum and other cookware are reactive and leach into the food.

5. Retain skins as much as possible, as all the nutrients are in the skin. Use a good vegetable brush to scrub them with water before using.

6. Plunge salad leaves into ice cold water before using them. It perks them up.

---

3) Good beans and luscious legumes

All beans have nourishing characteristics and are a great source of fibre as they contain only unsaturated fat, protein, folate, trace minerals, as well as all your B vitamins and they provide slow and steady energy which will strengthen blood quality. When combined with a whole grain, the protein quotient goes up to as much as that of what you would get from meat products, without the saturated fats or calories. They reduce the risk of heart disease, certain cancers, stabilize blood sugar levels, are low in glycemic load, lower cholesterol, and cure bone issues such as osteoporosis and arthritis.

In the Indian context, fresh whole beans include red kidney, whole green moong, and chowli. All whole beans when dried are called pulses. When pulses are split, they are termed as dals (the ones with an outer skin are nutritionally richer than the ones with no skin). Among beans, soybeans are best used when fermented to tofu and miso (as they are more digestible). We generally combine beans with tomatoes (Vitamin C), and this helps the body to absorb the iron in them better.

Most Indians suffer from 'beanophobia', and have no idea of what this wonderful food can do to them. I have many clients who have finally eaten their beans after years of keeping off them for fear of just one thing—'bad gas'. In all the years that I have stayed vegetarian, I have never been protein deficient and I exercise a lot, and have still maintained my muscle tone. Contrary to what people say that protein from a non-vegetarian source builds good muscle tone, I get all my protein from a vegetarian source.

#See Recipe section for delicious recipes on beans/legumes.

Tips on cooking beans to reduce gas

1. Whole beans must be soaked well, almost eight hours overnight (they are yang and by pre soaking them, we add a yin component to them, making them expand). Discard the water it's been soaked in; this eliminates the gas factor. You can also add warm water for about an hour till the beans swells up to twice its size; it keeps them firm and retains their shape when cooked.

2. If you feel you have problems associated with digesting beans, then pressure cook them, as this will make them more digestible.

3. Take off the foam as it cooks.

4. Add salt and any acid-forming ingredient like tomatoes, vinegar, but only at the end, as it prevents the bean from softening.

5. A Japanese sea vegetable called kombu* can be used; just add a stamp-size piece (when cooking for four people) when you begin to cook your beans or dals and remove the kombu once the beans have been cooked and the tempering is done. This will soften the beans and make their protein and fat more digestible. Kombu also adds trace minerals to your food, pushing up the health quotient of your meal.

6. To sweeten them, add large amounts of sweet vegetables like red pumpkin (bhopla), carrots, and onions while they cook, and less water.

*Kombu is available in speciality stores in larger cities or you can check for availability online.

Tip to enhance the taste of the bean

This method is referred to as the 'shock method'. For ½ cup of beans, take 1¼ cup water to cook them. Once the beans reach a boiling point, cover slightly and add cold water from the side, then cover again. You can repeat this till the beans are almost cooked. Once they are done, add your seasonings or tempering.

---

4) Fantastic Fermented Foods

Most of us have killed off all our good stomach bacteria without realizing it, which means we've compromised our ability to digest foods and absorb essential vitamins. A few weeks of heavy drinking, both alcohol and coffee, and diet rich in refined carbohydrates, sugar, and often lacking soluble fibre, is all it takes to throw the good bacteria in your gut into a frenzy. Another common cause of bacterial imbalances comes from heavy dozes of antibiotics and pain relieving medications—these kill everything in sight, including your beneficial intestinal bacterial. Hence, after a major surgery and heavy medication, there is a loss of appetite indicating the presence of bad bacteria in the body. The outcome? A digestive system that no longer functions effectively and an immune system now left weak, making you susceptible to colds, allergies, and flu's.

Discomfort after eating food, bloating, headache, constipation, diarrhea, urinary tract infections, thrush, and acne are all warning signs that your good bacteria are getting depleted and being replaced by bad bacteria. Modern medicine has very little to offer when this happens. Traditional Chinese Medicine and Ayurveda have been advocating what modern medicine is now beginning to accept—that a shortage of 'good' bacteria in the gastrointestinal tract (GI) can affect nearly every system in the body, from respiratory to digestion. Candidiasis, the overgrowth of candida (fungus; genus of yeasts; unfriendly microorganisms), is not a disease but a condition indicating an inner imbalance. Its symptoms are usually hidden or accompany other diseases. When the immune system is weak, candida invades the intestinal tract, sinuses, vagina, and shows up on your tongue. Donna Gates, who founded the Body Ecology Diet based on clearing candida from the body, describes it as a carpet-like mass which warps around your spinal cord, burrows itself in all your organs, and accumulates in your brain. It can accumulate around your heart and liver and is one of the main causes for reproductive issues and endometriosis in women, since the uterus is where mucous generally accumulates as it is an open area.

When it comes to losing weight, you first want a clean digestive tract; as good digestive energy gives your body more energy to lose weight, and your organs process better. The goal is to get rid of bad bacteria floating around and ingest yourself with good bacteria daily; also not eat foods that will multiply the bad bacteria like dairy, sugar, alcohol, and animal foods (meats).

Fermented foods are powerful as they supply you with rich microorganisms (good bacteria) that aid digestion and strengthen immunity. The age-old process of fermentation serves two functions (1) preservation (2) making food more digestible. Fermentation creates new nutrients as well like B vitamins, folic acid, riboflavin, niacin, thiamin, biotin, and B12. They are antioxidants by nature and are also know to create Omega 3. The bottom line is that you enhance the nutrition quotient of your meal by taking in good fermented foods on the side.

Probiotic food has huge immune-boosting powers. These not only help you sail past colds and fevers, but also prevent the growth of excess candida in the digestive tract, banish bloating and bad skin. These can be found not only in supplements but also through food.

Replenishing good bacteria must be done daily and should be constant in our daily diets. Kimchi, miso, probiotic drinks such as lassi, fermented vegetables (quick pickles), and brown rice idlis are all foods high in probiotics. Supplements also contain a wide spectrum of strains, which could help to step up the digestive system. **The trick to achieving inner health is to replenish your body's levels of good bacteria on a regular basis, while avoiding foods that feed bad bacteria.** In the short term, probiotics (through good fermented food), whether in the form of a pill or a drink, are a great tool. If you suffer from a seriously bad digestive situation, you will need to cut out bread, yeast, sugar, and fermented foods, as well as alcohol for some time. Once the body picks up, and you support it with good bacteria foods, you will see a lot of change.

Indian foods have a wide variety of fermented foods; yoghurt, buttermilk, and idlis are a few. Indian pickles however don't qualify as they contain too many yang ingredients which may enhance flavour of the meal, but will contract you. Pickles made the Indian way are greasy and fermented for extremely long periods with a lot of salt; this will produce a yang condition and make you tight and contracted from inside.

So eat them in moderation. I recommend a quicker versions of our Indian pickles, made in salt water brine, for example, in the Pressed Salad recipe (see p 279), the salt and the fermentation process changes the natural sugars in the vegetables to lactic acid, which strengthens your inner ecosystem. I also recommend adding miso to soups and dals, pressing vegetables (as a side salad), and making some quick pickles.

#See Recipe section for good fermented food recipes

What is Miso?

Miso is a soybean fermented paste originating in China some 2500 years ago. It is fermented with salt and grains for six months to a year. They come in many varieties and colours. For India, I recommend the lighter version to start with, and then slowly graduating to the darker version.

Usually referred to as 'the Silver Bullet', miso contains an anticancer agent called genistein, a plant isoflavone. Miso has twenty times more isoflavones (phytochemicals that act as antioxidants) than any other unfermented soy foods. The fermentation provides us with lactobacilli, increasing the quantity, availability, digestibility, and assimilability of nutrients while promoting a healthy pH balance in the digestive system. It has a trace of Vitamin

B12 and helps flush out fat and excess oil used for cooking. It also helps people balance out the negatives of an animal food diet.

I recommend using miso in soups and dals (beans) (see Recipe section).

6

FOODS TO CHANGE
YOUR MOODS

I was an angry child. I couldn't reign in my temper and had no control over my speech. My very dear friend still reminds me of our first meeting, and says that I not only came across as a harsh person, but was terribly unpleasant. The twenties are always a hard time. It's when you turn into an adult and start shouldering responsibilities. For me, it was a particularly rough period. And to add to it, I had bad eating habits. I had blood sugar swings which affected my mood, and all the dairy I consumed slowed me down. I had hypoglycemia, which is indicative of the spleen/pancreas being completely out of shape. The spleen/pancreas are governed by anxiety and worry (see chart depicting organs and corresponding emotions and foods)— both emotions were predominant in my life. I fuelled this with coffee and sugar every day. No matter how much I meditated, by midday these emotions were back and stayed with me till I went to bed. I suffered from lack of sleep, and my diet was not helping either. I was eating dead foods and this reflected in everything, including the way I looked.

Like the lotus root example (see p 101) and how it helps with its own life force to help your life force, foods which are dead (out of a box like bread, cookies or sugar, excessive cheese) will also bring in their own characters, adding different dimensions to you and your mind.

WHAT ARE 'LIVING FOODS'?

Fresh foods are living foods because they have energy, and in turn give us energy. Whole foods retain their living energy up to a point when cooked too. These living foods carry chi, prana, or life force, which affects our life force. They contain a wide range of vital nutrients (vitamins, minerals, amino acids, oxygen) and live enzymes, which have not been destroyed by processing. Their nutritional properties are essential to the proper maintenance of human bodily functions.

We must not confuse living foods with raw foods. Some health experts advocate that cooking vegetables destroys their nutritional properties. Wrong! Cooking adds energy to the food and enhances its properties for better assimilation and digestion. Our task is to use these 'living foods', and by employing the right cooking styles, we can increase the quality of nutrients that are absorbed from food, and influence the energy needed at a particular time. For example, would you say that corn flakes, touting bran flakes on the box and fortified with vitamins, is live food when compared to brown rice poha? Obviously the distinction is quite clear—poha is the live food.

Bran flakes are dead as they have been processed, fortified, and then packaged.

EXAMPLES OF LIVING FOODS:

Whole grains: Brown rice, millet, whole wheat, barley, buckwheat (kuttu ka atta)
Beans: Split dals, red/black/white kidney beans, green moong, chowli, soybeans (all whole or split beans)
Vegetables: Round, root, and leafy greens
Fruit: All
Seeds: Pumpkin, sesame, flax, sunflower
Nuts: Walnuts, almonds, peanuts, cashews, pistachios
Good quality fermented foods: quick pickles, miso, tofu, idlis, home-made probiotic drinks, and yoghurt (made from non-dairy source preferable)

Structurally, the human brain resembles your stomach, and just like your brain comprises nerves, blood, and bone, the enteric nervous system is the brain in the gut. The gut is smarter than you know. And like the larger brain in the head, this system sends and receives impulses, records experiences, and responds to emotions. The enteric nervous system is located in the sheaths of tissue lining the esophagus, stomach, small intestine, and colon. Its nerve cells are bathed and influenced by the same neurotransmitters that influence your brain. The gut can upset the brain just as the brain can upset the gut.

The gut plays a vital role in your happiness and misery. We rely upon our *gut instinct* or *gut reaction* to point us in the right direction. Think about it, when you are faced with intense fear or panic, it can bring about a queasy feeling in the stomach or even nausea. All my clients with gastrointestinal problems are very stressed in their minds, which in turn affects their stomachs. The kind of foods you eat can change the environment within your first and second brain. **What you need to do is feed your brain and organs food for your moods.** But before that you need to understand what neurotransmitters are. The real challenge in altering your moods is how you can enhance the quality of neurotransmitters through foods that work.

The brain needs neurotransmitters such as seratonin, dopamine, and norepinephrine—a range of brain chemicals that are the mediators for your moods. Let's have a look at them:

Neurotransmitter	Positives	Negatives
Seratonin	Sense of security, well being, confidence	Moody, depressive, aggressive, low self esteem and energy, confusion, low sex drive, sense of unworthiness
Dopamine	Strength, vitality, energy	Lethargy, weakness. Excess dopamine leads to anxiety and fear.
Norepinephrine	Good flight/fight reactions	Same as dopamine

When I started eating the right foods and did away with the ones that inhibited the supply of these neurotransmitters, I immediately started feeling happier and hence healthier. My gut was happy and my 'gut feelings' were usually correct. Essentially what I did was cut back the high stress foods from my diet and started adding good wholesome foods—it was really that simple. My moods, emotions, and habit patterns took some time to shift, but shift they did. For the better. My blood sugar levels stabilized, I lost weight, didn't crave sugar, and got my energy back.

Foods that help to release neurotransmitters

Most people get their serotonin fix, albeit temporarily, from the wrong foods. People who are generally low in serotonin are also somewhat depressive and their need would then be to satisfy themselves with carbohydrate-rich foods—the wrong kind. It cuts out on the depressed state but only for a little bit. It comes back again, as your spleen and pancreas get thrown off with the sugar, creating those spikes in insulin levels and makes you want more of the sugary stuff.

FOODS THAT SPEED UP NEUROTRANSMITTERS
TEMPORARILY, THEN CAUSE THEM TO DIP

Coffee, Indian tea, sugar, processed carbohydrates, sodas, colas, and chocolates.

The trick is to switch to whole grains, legumes and beans, fruits and vegetables, which give you the sustained sugars and tryptophan (an amino acid) which is necessary for the release of serotonin. Among vegetables, focus on the starchy variety, which are richer in tryptophan, as they boost serotonin faster than low starch vegetables.

> **FIX YOUR GUT, FIX YOUR MOOD**
>
> Your gut produces about 95 percent of the body's supply of serotonin, which regulates brain functions such as sleep and moods. When your gut is troubled, it communicates its unhappiness to the brain.

Norepinephrine and dopamine get boosted by protein foods. The amino acid tyrosine from protein foods gets converted to dopamine in the brain. The table below highlights foods that boost these neurotransmitters.

Neurotransmitters	Corresponding Foods
	WHOLE GRAINS
	Millets, brown rice, barley, quinoa, whole oats (not rolled), whole wheat, corn, amaranth, and all other whole grains
SERATONIN	**VEGETABLES**
	Starchy vegetables
	All beans and legumes
DOPAMINE	Protein-rich foods like fish, chicken, turkey, legumes (beans and all dals), soy fermented products such as tofu
NOREPINEPHRINE	
#Nuts, seeds, and green or herbal teas affect all	

Your lifestyle activities also affect neurotransmitters. While walking, stretching, pilates, dancing are all serotonin boosters, aerobics, jogging, gymming, swimming, and playing tennis will reduce dopamine/noreprinephrine temporarily and increase serotonin for that time. Anything competitive will increase dopamine and norepinephrine. Music also changes the moods and different types of music releases different neurotransmitters. As does writing, which is a great serotonin booster. Traditional Chinese Medicine also says that each organ is affected by emotions both positive and negative, and foods you eat will either nourish your organs and emotions positively or impact them negatively. For example, if you are an anxious and worried person, you are likely to throw you spleen and pancreas off—this is how I was, so I ended up developing hypo-glycemia. The foods I ate (like sugar, processed food) fuelled this pattern. Eventually, whole natural living foods got me out of this vicious circle.

Foods that feed your organs, emotions, and moods— Within the Traditional Chinese Medicine system, each organ is viewed as a complex energetic system encompassing not only its anatomical entity, but also correlated with a particular emotion. So if we take the kidneys, they are governed by fear and insecurity. Usually people who push themselves with work, lifestyle, diet, and are constantly plugged into fear will burn out their adrenals (adrenals sit on top of the kidneys). Apart from a diet rich in whole grains, legumes, vegetables, good quality fermented foods and minus the processed foods, sugar, dairy, animal foods (meats)—a brief description of what works for each organ is given below.

Organs	Foods that Feed Each Organ/Emotion	Foods That Harm Each Organ
Liver Anger Impatience	Barley, oats (whole), wheat, rye; all upward growing plants; lentils; good quality fermented foods; a sour taste such as lime; turmeric, basil, cardamom, cumin, ginger, mint leaves, strawberries; cabbage, cauliflower, turnips, broccoli; all sprouted grains; all bitter foods such as arugula leaves, fenugreek; amaranth (rajgeera), quinoa, radish and radish leaves; all chlorophyll-rich palnts; spirulina; while cooking, use active upward movement cooking styles like light	Oily greasy foods (fat), saturated fats from animal foods (including dairy), eggs; alcohol
Heart Not Joyful	All whole grains (esp. amaranth), brown rice; buckwheat (kuttu ka atta); legumes (esp. soybeans), sprouts; pungent foods such as radish, onion, garlic; leafy greens, broccoli, cabbage, asparagus, cucumbers, parsley (rich in magnesium, helps absorb calcium and restrains anxiety), spirulina; seeds such as chia	Tobacco, coffee, refined salt, sugar, refined flour, all intoxicants, excessive protein, spicy foods, rich food, large dinners, late-night eating

	(subja), flax, sunflower, walnuts, pumpkin, jujube (ber); fish; raw honey; mushrooms; fruit: like berries, lemons, mandarin; herbs such as dill (suha), basil, chamomile (babunphul), catnip (fudina); ghee	
Spleen/ Pancreas Anxiety Worry	Whole grains like brown rice, foxtail millet (well cooked); high starchy veggies like red pumpkin (lal kaddu), carrots, turnip, sweet potatoes; legumes (esp. black beans), chickpeas; pungent vegetables like onions, leeks, ginger; spices such as fennel, nutmeg, cinnamon, garlic; fish	Restrict raw vegetables, fruit and juices, sprouts, too much fibre, spinach, and tomatoes, if really weak in these organs; also avoid dairy; large and rich greasy meals; nuts, seeds, yeast or yeasted products, sugars, animal foods, overeating
Lungs Depression Grief	All pungent foods like onions, radish, mustard; help discharge mucous cabbage; greens like arugula; beta-carotene rich foods like carrot, red pumpkin; peppers; broccoli, parsley, turnips, wheat grass, greens—as chlorophyll helps lungs discharge toxins; spirulina; fruits	Too much dairy and dairy products, sugar, cigarettes, processed foods, refined salt, meats

	(esp. yellow-orange variety); fibre-rich foods clean lungs; all whole grains; vegetables like lotus root, all root vegetables	
Kidneys Fear Insecurity	Magnesium-rich foods help calm nerves (see foods mentioned in heart foods); whole grains like millet, barley, buckwheat (kuttu ka atta); tofu; all beans (esp. soybean); watermelons, melons; wheat germ; spirulina; black sesame; wheat grass; ghee; almond milk; royal jelly	Salty and bitter foods, eggs, animal foods, cheese

THE MAGICAL L-TRYPTOPHAN

L-tryptophan is an amino acid that has been taken widely to promote a calm mind, sound sleep, and reduce anxiety and depression. As mentioned earlier, it is serotonin which needs tryptophan at its foundation. Tryptophan should actually come out of food, where it is not synthetically generated. A diet rich in animal foods or too much protein will inhibit the formation of tryptophan (as amino acids from the protein compete with it). Our bodies only need small amounts of tryptophan to aid with serotonin production. A diet which is rich in animal foods (namely animal protein), has a reverse effect on tryptophan production. The amino acids in the animal foods like dairy and meats in high protein diets compete with the use of tryptophan (also an amino acid) in the formation of serotonin. A safer way to get tryptophan is through plant-based foods. Research has shown that high carbohydrate diets enhance the presence of tryptophan in the brain. That's why it is called a Sattvic diet with the following food categories: whole grains, vegetables, fruits, lentils, beans; which also emphasizes complex carbohydrates and is very close to this approach and promotes brain chemistry which is rich in tryptophan.

FOODS THAT MAKE YOU TENSE

Certain foods like cheese, eggs, salt, baked products, chips, chivdas, and roasted products will make you feel tensed, stuck, dry, very thirsty, lethargic, irritated, and heavy.

To feel relaxed, calm, open to new thoughts, and energized, eat steamed/boiled vegetables, raw salad, corn (as a whole or made into rotis), fruits, whole grains like brown rice (boiled), millet, quinoa, fish (non vegetarian), or a pasta made from whole grain.

FOODS THAT CAUSE MOOD SWINGS

Foods like coffee, milk, alcohol, sugar, any preservatives in food, a lot of fruit or fruit juices, too much yoghurt, raw salad, tomatoes, or spices will cause mood swings, tiredness, scattered in your thoughts, confused, and directionless.

To help feel clear headed, decisive, devoid of any sharp mood swings, calm, and steadfast, have foods like whole grains (pressure cooked), round and root vegetables, leafy greens, soup (with miso), fish, desserts with the right natural sweetener, and roasted nuts.

To utilize the protein from your food, make adjustments in the mental patterns which affect your organs. The liver, spleen, pancreas, and stomach must be strengthened to make the body use protein efficiently. This will not only bring about weight loss, it will also keep your liver healthy.

A few ways to stay stress free:

1. Try to breathe deeply when faced with stressful situations. Tell yourself that this feeling will pass.
2. Work during work hours, and relax during your free time.
3. Exercise regularly.
4. Avoid the intake of greasy foods, stimulants, sugars, coffees, and excessive fruit.
5. Consuming small portions of food containing protein are better than having large portions.
6. Chew, chew, chew.

FLAVOURS, ORGANS, AND THEIR CORRESPONDING EFFECTS

Organs	Liver	Heart	Spleen/ Pancreas	Lungs/ Large Intestine	Kidneys/ Sex organs
Tastes	Sour	Bitter	Sweet	Pungent	Salty

Flavours enhance a meal, but the Beauty Diet uses flavours to benefit a particular organ. For example, when I cook for someone who has a liver imbalance, I make sure that their food has all the flavours, but that it is predominantly sour. So I use lime (in a salad or given on the side) or the right quality vinegar (in salad dressings). Liver imbalances precede a weight issue, so I use the sour flavour which will not only nourish the liver, but also add a sweet flavour as most imbalances in the body stem from the spleen/pancreas being out of balance.

At times, one particular flavour can be used to balance out many organs. For example, a salty flavour (not using table salt, but rock or sea salt and gomashio) sorts out imbalances in the kidney, and at the same time, it also benefits the spleen and pancreas, strengthens digestion and your heart, and improves concentration.

So how do you go about figuring which flavour to use when? Here's how. Take your main dish and think of the one flavour you would like to bring out in that dish. This flavour should balance your entire meal. So if it's sweet for that day, use sweet vegetables and pull back on the spices and salt, and then step it up with some mild herbs such as basil. The other dishes will feature the remaining flavours (but played down) like pungent, bitter, and salty (see chart on p 129 for foods pertaining to each flavour).

SALTY

Each flavour adds the yang and yin element (comparatively) to your meal. So a salt is yang (see chart on p 21), but when the right kind of salt is used and in the right amount, it will actually cool you instead of contracting you (that is, dehydrate you), unless you have it in excess. A salty flavour has the ability to dissolve hard structures like cysts and tissues in the body. According to the Ayurvedic tradition, salt lubricates tissues and stimulates digestion.

This flavour strengthens your stomach (as it will impact your spleen/pancreas), thus affecting other organs such as the kidneys and heart.

Bitter

A bitter flavour is cooling in nature, and the energy, instead of rising, goes downward into the body. And since it is cooling, it works well for people who have an aggressive disposition. It's a flavour that works positively for your heart, as it helps to clean it up by dissolving the fats around the heart. Mustard leaves are a very good example of the kind of bitter I'm talking about. The bitter flavour also helps to detoxify the liver, and is excellent while on a weight-loss plan or for someone with skin issues, candida, or mucous in the system. The kidneys and lungs also benefit from a bitter flavour, and it is ideal for someone with a mucous condition in the lungs. Dandelion (baunphal) or liquorice (mulethi) tea will be helpful in such a case. In the Ayurvedic tradition, this flavour detoxifies and lightens tissues.

Sweet

The liver, spleen, pancreas, and stomach work together. An imbalanced liver affects the stomach functions, causing abdominal inflammation, gas and indigestion, and conditions like colitis and other digestive disorders. A sweet flavour (from whole living foods like complex carbohydrates) moves your energy up and disperses it outward. It relaxes you, thereby calming your digestive system. While benefitting your spleen/pancreas, it also affects the 'angry' liver by making it happy. One of the best ways to cure a liver is to also nourish it with a sweet flavour (but only the good kind of sweets, mind you), as it releases some of the built-up excess. According to the Ayurvedic tradition, a sweet flavour builds tissues and calms the nerves. So your overtly anxious and worried mind will be calmed. People on a weight-loss programme, however, must limit the sweet flavour by reducing the amount of complex carbohydrates they take in.

PUNGENT

Think of what happens when you have wasabi or mustard. It stings your nose, opening it up and clearing up your sinuses. The effect is warm and energy rushes upward and outward. A pungent flavour benefits the lungs and large intestine as it helps to stimulate the circulation of blood and energy, enhancing digestion, as well as breaking up mucous caused by dairy and animal foods. The extra circulation also helps the heart. It gives a push to the liver if it is in a stagnant mode, and will also tone the entire fluid structure of the body (which is ruled by the kidneys). So in general, a little pungency can get your mood going! In the Ayurvedic tradition, it stimulates digestion and metabolism. A stronger pungent flavour, almost astringent, such as from white or red radish, will help dry out fats, and reduce water in the body.

SOUR

A sour flavour acts as a cleaning agent for your liver, cleansing the build up of excessive fats. It helps to digest foods and improves the absorption of minerals, making your lungs stronger. In the Ayurvedic tradition, a sour flavour cleans out tissues and increases mineral absorption, which sharpens your senses.

Flavours	Natural Foods
Salt	Refined, rock, sea salt; miso; soy sauce; all seaweed like spirulina and kombu; millet, barley; pickles; gomasio (recipe in salt section of book), fish
Bitter	Arugula leaves, celery, romaine lettuce, alfalfa; dark chocolate; sauerkraut; turmeric, fenugreek; gourd; baunphal (dandelion), grapefruit, olives, bitter melon; bitter & sweet asparagus; amaranth; papaya; bitter gourd (karela); curry leaves, rye seeds, bay leaves (tej patta), neem leaves, liquorice root (mulethi); stevia; some vinegars; wine
Sweet	Carbohydrates like sweet rice (brown); all fruits; natural sugars; dairy products; vegetables like cabbage, red pumpkin, onions, mushrooms (shiitake), beetroots, cucumber, eggplant, sweet potato, carrots, celery, (sometimes sweet and bitter), spinach; red beans (adzuki), saffron, all natural sweeteners, date, raisins; honey;, cinnamon (dalchini), lavender, nutmeg (jaiphal); almonds, walnuts, sesame/sunflower seeds; coconut; sugar
Sour	Sour fruits like strawberry, kiwi, litchi, lemons, limes, all citrus fruits; fermented foods like yoghurt, sauerkraut; sour apples; all vinegars; grapes, mangoes, oranges, tomatoes; naturally fermented bread (sourdough)
Pungent	Peppers, chilli, herbs, garlic, spices, white/red radish, leek; green onions,

Astringent	Turnip, ginger, peppermint, black pepper, clove, dill, parsley, fennel (saunf), ginger, mustard; legumes (beans/lentils); pears, pomegranate; dried fruit, asparagus, turnip; coffee, tea; rye; buckwheat (kuttu), quinoa

Make a meal plan that uses all flavours, but with one flavour dominating the meal. Make sure you get a taste of all flavours at least once during the day, because if you don't, you will end up craving them in some other unhealthy form. Your cravings will be greatly reduced by following this principle.

Meal plans for different emotions and moods

Here are five basic menu plans for one day which include breakfast, lunch, and dinner. They have been prepared in such a way as to feed each organ and help change your moods. With their help, you can practically experience the effects of these foods and how one orchestrates them in a meal plan.

1) THE SETTLING-AND-CENTRING MENU PLAN

Menu for spleen/pancreas: For when you are feeling anxious, worried, tensed, and stuck in some thought pattern and want to feel relaxed, light, have more clarity in your thoughts.

Breakfast:
- Use millet (cheena) to make a porridge. Layer it with apples if you want a sweet taste or red pumpkin if you can take a salty flavour

OR

- Choose a gluten-free flour (as gluten will pull you down) like sorghum (jowar) or amaranth (rajgeera). Add some grated red pumpkin to it and make rotis to eat with chutney (green coriander with mint)
- Chamomile tea

Lunch:
- Brown rice (pressure cooked)
- Chickpeas with greens
- Glazed carrots

Mid afternoon/early evening:
- Sweet vegetable drink
- Sweet potato chaat

Dinner:
- Round vegetable soup
- Cabbage pressure cooked with spices
- Yellow lentils (any) boiled and cooked with a cubed squash
- If you haven't had millet (cheena) in the morning then have it here as a grain

OR

- Sorghum (jowar rotis)/amaranth (rotis with a leafy green like fenugreek or spinach)

2) THE COMPLETE-LIVER-FLUSH MENU PLAN

Menu plan for liver/gall bladder: For when you are angry,

agitated, feeling unfriendly and disappointed and want to feel less angry, patient, friendly, and satisfied.

Breakfast:

- Whole oats porridge worked in the same way like the brown rice porridge

OR

- Wheat rotis with some leafy greens (spinach or fenugreek) and a chutney (tamarind/date chutney)
- Green tea

Lunch:

- White bean salad
- Cabbage in green sauce
- Barley mushroom risotto

OR

- Wheat rotis or gluten-free flour rotis

Mid afternoon/early evening:

- Make a snack with 1½ cup finely chopped broccoli, pak choi, parsley, and green onions and simmer with 1 cup of water for 5 minutes. Cool and blend in a mixer, drink as a mid-afternoon liver booster
- Endive salad with nuts and a dash of lime

Dinner:

- Broccoli soup
- Any split lentil with tempering (use turmeric, cumin, and ginger for sure)

- Millet whole grain or rotis
- A leafy green veggie such as spinach or fenugreek and some sauerkraut on the side

3) THE HAPPY-GO-LUCKY MENU PLAN

Menu plan for lungs/large intestine: For when you are feeling sad, depressed, overwhelmed and want to feel happy, empowered, and energetic.

Breakfast:

- Brown rice porridge

  OR

- Brown rice rotis with leafy greens and chutney with ginger or mustard
- Herbal tea

Lunch:

- Brown rice (boiled)
- Pumpkin seed and cashew curry with carrot chutney made with mustard
- White soybean salad with mustard dressing

  OR

- White bean salad

Mid afternoon/early evening:

- Lotus root tea
- Stewed apple/pear

Dinner:
- Broccoli soup
- Quinoa or millet with carrots and leafy greens

OR

- Rotis
- Yellow split lentils with lotus root (stir fried) added towards the end and tempered with mustard seeds (add curry leaves and spices)

4) THE GETTING-IT-TOGETHER MENU PLAN

Menu for the heart/small intestine: For when you are feeling overworked, tensed, full of scattered energy and want to feel gathered, calm, and lighter.

Breakfast:
- Quinoa or millet porridge

OR

- Amaranth rotis
- Leafy greens

OR

- Amaranth flour idlis/dosa with chutney (make sure you add turmeric, celery, and methi seeds while tempering it)
- Tulsi tea

Lunch:
- Amaranth rotis with arugula or mustard leaves

OR

- Millet whole grain with red kidney bean curry (like rajma)
- Any good seasonal leafy green (mustard)

OR

- A salad with arugula
- White radish pickle (if handy)

Mid afternoon/early evening:
- A bowl of any kind of mellon, berries, or summer fruit

OR

- Buckwheat (kuttu) dhoklas
- Tulsi or chamomile tea

Dinner:
- Broccoli soup (½ a white radish). Keep the grain light, so if you have not had the millet earlier, do so now

OR

- Amaranth rotis with white beans in a gravy
- Cucumber salad with dill (suha) and other herbs

5) THE BE-BOLD MENU PLAN

Menu plan for kidneys/bladder: For when you are feeling fearful, insecure, and overwrought and want to feel secure, confident, fearless, and bold.

Breakfast:
- Dhoklas made with buckwheat (kuttu)

  OR

- Whole oats porridge

Lunch:
- Brown rice (pressure cooked)

  OR

- Millet whole grain
- White soybean (protein) salad, Black bean salad (p 278) or black bean (cooked in a curry)
- Okra stew

Mid afternoon/early evening:
- Dried fruits
- Green, tulsi, or any other herbal tea

Dinner:
- Soybean soup
- Vary the grain; use buckwheat in roti, brown rice, or millet
- Cooked black lentils
- Spinach or broccoli steamed with lemon tahini sauce

7

THE ESSENTIAL
SHOPPING GUIDE

If you've paid attention to the previous chapters, you will have emptied your larder and fridge of all those no no's. The jams, mayonnaise in jars, sweetened fruit juices, corn flakes, sausages. If you haven't, there's still enough time to rehaul and restock with the good stuff, the living foods, that will set you on the path to a better gut and a happier and healthier you. So what are you waiting for?

A note on organic food

The big question. To go organic or not. For the vast majority of human history, agriculture can be described as organic. Only during the twentieth century was a large supply of new synthetic chemicals introduced to the food supply. Organic is simply defined as food that is farmed without the use of pesticides, antibiotics, or genetically manufactured organisms (GMOs).

Organically grown fruits and vegetables have significantly higher levels of antioxidants than traditionally cultivated food products. And because organically grown fruits and vegetables are higher in antioxidants, these items reduce the risk of certain types of cancers. Antioxidants also have a restorative effect on skin and muscle deterioration. Foods that are high in antioxidants help to slow down the ageing process by inhibiting the deterioration of muscles and skin.

Phytonutrients, nutrients derived from plant material and proved to be necessary for sustaining human life, are higher in organic produce because crops rely more on their own defenses in the absence of regular applications of chemical pesticides. For example, levels of lycopene, an antioxidant found in tomatoes, is higher in organic tomatoes, and polyphenols (antioxidants that help to protect you against ageing) are higher in organic potatoes.

If you want to ensure that the foods you consume on a regular basis will promote good health, turn to organic food products or include more of them in your daily diet. Look at it as a preventive tool towards serious diseases such as cancer and other major health issues.

We all know that pesticides by their very nature are toxic. It is no rocket science that if chemicals can be harmful and have the power to kill living creatures in plants, they can also harm us. Pesticides, herbicides, genetically modified foods, and growth hormones all lessen the nutritive value in food. The medicinal value of organic products is of particular benefit for people suffering from serious health concerns, where the body is already toxic from within. Would I say it's better even for normal, healthy people to opt for organic food? Yes. If you can, please do. But in India we face legitimate issues with getting organic produce, especially vegetables, so it may be an arduous process. If you can't go 100 percent organic, try and do as much as you can to benefit from the process.

Now let's shop!

The recommended shopping list

WHOLE GRAINS AND GRAIN PRODUCTS

- Brown rice (Long grain and short grain)
- Foxtail millet (Yellow millet, also called cheena)
- All grain (flours as well), also referred to as millet: sorghum (jowar), nachni, barley or pearl millet (jov), buckwheat (kuttu), finger millet (ragi) and amaranth (rajgeera), quinoa (available in speciality stores only)
- Noodles: Udon, Soba (usually buckwheat). Noodles in the Indian market are made from refined flour, udon is made from 100 percent whole wheat or any other whole wheat pasta, and soba from 100 percent buckwheat (kuttu)

A NOTE ON BREAD

All bread available in the Indian market has yeast and maida (in different proportions), and both these ingredients cause nothing but harm to the body. White bread is a strict no-no. If you can't keep bread out of your life, go for whole wheat unyeasted breads.

VEGETABLES AND FRUITS

- All kinds including dark leafy greens
- Among fruits, limit bananas if you suffer from bronchial issues, as they are mucous causing. However, bananas are an excellent source of potassium and are your best bet if you are lacking in potassium. Potassium deficiency can be detected via a blood test. Symptoms could range from muscle cramps, fatigue, irregular heartbeat, thirst, mood swings, irritability, low blood pressure, and insomnia. People at risk are those on high sodium diets, or those who are constantly dieting. People who have used laxatives for a long duration, those under a lot of stress, and older people may also be deficient in potassium.

BEANS AND BEAN PRODUCTS

- All whole beans such as red kidney, chickpeas (kabuli channa), bengal gram (black channa), chickpea green (cholia/green channa), black-eyed beans (chowli); and any other legumes
- Soya products such as soya granules, nuggets, tofu (also called soya paneer)

ABOUT SOY AND ITS PRODUCTS

Both soy and soy isoflavones have many health benefits, including prevention of cardiovascular disease, cancer, and osteoporosis, as well as treatment of menopausal symptoms. Soy provides a complete source of dietary protein, and unlike most plant proteins, it contains all the essential amino acids.

However, it best to limit soy intake to small portions, up to three times a week. Don't make it a mainstay in your diet. Those on a weight-loss programme should avoid soy milk completely.

Fish

- All kinds except salmon and shellfish (during weight loss)

Seeds and nuts

- Sesame, sunflower, pumpkin, walnuts, and almonds

Condiments and seasonings

- Sea or rock salt
- Ginger
- Garlic
- Natural mustard
- Herbs (all kinds)
- All Indian spices

Spread and Jams

- Tahini (sesame butter)
- Unsweetened jams (read labels)

Sweeteners

- Stevia
- Apple juice
- Pure maple syrup

BEVERAGES

- Herbal and decaffeinated teas
- Apple juice

SNACKS

- Unsweetened granola
- Whole wheat crackers
- Rice cakes
- Toasted seeds such as pumpkin, popcorn, raisins (mounaka raisins)
  (See snack section)

Note: Never buy readymade spreads. Make your peanut butter, hummus, and baba ghanoush at home. Fruit-made sweeteners can also be made by pulping fruit to use as sweeteners in your desserts. Also make all fruit and vegetable juices fresh.

8

MEAL PLANNING AND HEALTHY SNACKING

How to plan a balanced meal?

Balancing a meal is extremely important to maintain good health, lose weight, reverse health conditions, and nourish yourself. Balance comes through regularity in meal timings, sitting down to eat calmly, combining the right kinds of food, chewing the food properly, and even the presentation of the meal.

As I've mentioned before, planning is the key to healthy eating habits. If you have your breakfast or lunch ready, there is no reason for you to go down to the cafeteria and eat outside or eat processed food. It's as simple and logical as that.

THE MUST-FOLLOW MEAL FLOWCHART

Your meal should follow this pattern:

The opening act: Soup
(for at least one meal of the day)
↓
The main actor: Whole grain
(what you should plan every meal around)
↓
The supporting actors: Two vegetables
(out of which one should be a green vegetable)
↓
The props: Legumes
(or fish for non vegetarians)
↓
The director: Good quality fermented foods
(the glue which holds your meal together)

BREAKFAST

Breakfast literally means 'breaking the fast'. This vital meal sets the tone for your day. So you need foods which will give you sustained sugars and which will digest well and keep you feeling whole for the day. Whole grain, in any form, is your answer. We're looking at poha, rotis, porridge, dosas, idlis.

Plan the night before. If it's porridge, brown rice, or whole oats, these grains will need to be soaked. If it's idli, you need to prepare two days ahead. Of course you're probably thinking she's a chef and she runs her own food business—what would she know what it's like to be on the run. Actually I do. Let me tell you my own experience.

I get up at 5.30 am and start my kitchen by 6 am. The kitchen is ready by 7 am (by which time the head chef has already started putting things together). To avoid keeping my stomach empty for too long, since the best time for breakfast is between 7 am and 9 am, I always grab some nuts, maybe 2–3 almonds or walnuts. I also make my poha or idlis the night before, as my kitchen runs till 9.30 am for morning meals. Around 7.30 am, I eat a bowl of poha or idlis or brown rice porridge. I do this while I'm in the kitchen, cooking or supervising my staff. I know I have to be on my feet, but eat I must.

If you plan it, there is a good chance you will not grab the easy stuff like commercial bread, eggs, stuff out of a box like muesli (everyday), or nothing at all. Just fruit alone? Never. Too much concentrated sugar only first thing in the morning. Fruit or fruit juice as the only breakfast in the morning will cause you to be moody and destabilize your blood sugar for a good part of the morning. If you do eat fruit, then an hour and a half later eat a whole grain. However, my recommendation is to do it the other way around, the whole grain first, then the fruit an hour or so later.

Coffee and tea in the morning?

The body goes into hibernation and a dehydrated state at night. That is why we reach out for a bottle of water first thing in the morning. Indian chai is yang and it dries you out even more. Coffee, on the other hand, will give you that expansive feeling because it is a strong stimulant. So in the list of liquids, coffee and tea (Indian chai) would actually go down in priority. Herbal tea, a green drink (wheat grass or spirulina in water), or a vegetable juice should take over. I also advise this especially if you are on a weight-loss or getting-healthy plan (most imbalances in the body stem from here, and this is one sure shot way to control cravings as well).

Lunch

This is one meal with the highest chances of being taken for granted, since most of us are generally at the peak of our mental activity during this time. Home-cooked meals are the rule and there are no exceptions. The star of the meal should be whole grain, so if it cannot be a roti, dal, and vegetables, then put together a soup with vegetables, lentils, and a whole grain. Or if you want to eat salad once a week, then throw in cooked grain like brown rice or millet.

Dinner

Dinner is the time when your body needs to unwind after a hard day's work. This is also the one meal when we like to take it easy, indulge, and eat to our heart's content. But remember that just like you, your gut is also tired and is retiring for the day. So keep your food simple. A lot of my clients, in their endeavour to lose weight, keep the grain component of the meal for dinner time. If you've had whole grains in both your other meals, you can go ahead without it. However, keeping off the whole grain at dinner time is just a way of minimizing the grain component in your day, which does help when on a weight-loss plan. Make sure the concentrated protein element in your meal is present here.

EATING EVERY TWO HOURS OR THREE BALANCED MEALS?

Diet-induced thermogenesis or 'grazing' (eating every two hours) as it is called in the West, is a popular tool for weight loss. The reason this approach also emerged on the weight loss scene was because:

(a) it was used for diabetics to maintain their blood sugar levels.
(b) people started moving away from eating three basic, balanced meals a day.
(c) some overate at regular meals.

While this technique has helped many, you can also eat three meals and also take a snack between meals when you are hungry. Follow the approach I am putting forth in this book and make sure if it's for weight loss, you have some form of concentrated protein at each meal. If you are going to eat every two hours, please do the following:

1. See what your food choices are: it should not be processed foods like biscuits or toasts (made of white bread—maida). Instead go for a brown rice poha, whole wheat crackers with hummus, carrot sticks, and fruits (see snack section).
2. Chew. That's something that most people miss while 'grazing'.
3. If you tend to have maxi snacks, then have mini meals at meal time. So be mindful of the quantity consumed at those times.

The decision to have three meals a day, two meals a day, or 'graze' every two hours is entirely your call. My experience with this approach has shown me that if you eat a balanced breakfast, lunch, and dinner—then eating between meals is not necessary unless you get really hungry.

Keep it short and simple or KISS

Connie Arnold, a dear friend who was healed from a cancer called non-Hodgkin lymphoma by this diet, told me, 'Keep it short and simple.' The most important thing is to get the meal itself right, which means that you're feeding your body the right foods. Once you're comfortable with the basic format, which I'll repeat again—**whole grains, vegetables of which one is a green leafy, beans (or fish), some fermented food, condiments, and soups**—then you know what canvas you have to work with. Don't be tempted by those elaborate and lovely recipe books. Use basic seasonings initially, and make simpler versions of the grain and beans. Make fewer dishes. Once you get better, you can graduate to more sophisticated versions of those recipes.

FOOD COMBINATIONS

It's a good thing to know the principles of combining food—especially for people with sensitive tummies and those that are on a weight-loss programme. Don't get panicked about this, but be conscious of it. The brain has a way of staying wired to the principles of food combinations. The principles I put forth stem from the Traditional Chinese system and those put forth by Paul Pitchford and adapted to the Indian context. When you start making good food combinations, three things happen:

(1) Lesser putrefaction in the stomach because of which there will be fewer bad bacteria floating around and a reduced tendency to develop candida.

(2) A stronger digestive system.

(3) Weight loss—as the chance of you developing toxins as well as fat decreases.

8 TIPS FOR FOOD COMBINATIONS:

1. **Fruits must be eaten on an empty stomach first thing in the morning**: As I mentioned, acidic fruits (sour) can be combined with yoghurt (if you do it). Fruits digest first before anything else, and therefore clubbing them with other food items will always pose a problem.

2. Salty flavoured foods, like your soup (which will have some miso or salt), should be the first thing to be eaten in the meal because it stimulates digestive juices.

3. Concentrated protein foods must be eaten in small amounts.

FOOD COMBINATIONS TO AVOID GAS FORMATION

- •Grain with dairy or animal food (meats)
- •Fruit with grain
- Dairy with animal food (meat)
- Melons by themselves
- Fruit with vegetables
- Fruit with beans

---

4. **A meal should almost always start with a soup. After the soup, however, if you are eating a high protein food like meat, chicken, or fish—then this must be**

eaten after the soup, as they take a long time to digest and almost always eat them with a non-starchy vegetable, especially greens; it is advisable not to eat beans/legumes at the same time when eating animal foods (as stated). For proper digestion of the meal, try not eating a starchy food at the same time when eating meat, chicken, fish, or beans/legumes.

5. **Eat protein with green and non-starchy vegetables:** As I've mentioned earlier, greens benefit the liver where protein is metabolized, so they are necessary for optimum utilization of protein in your body. For example, fish with steamed, stir-fried, or sautéed greens or saag; chicken with leafy green vegetables or vegetable soup (non-starchy vegetables).

6. **Eat whole grains and starchy vegetables with non-starchy vegetables:** All grains assimilate better when eaten with non-starchy or low-starch vegetables (each starch has a different digestion time). For example, have brown rice with either red pumpkin (bhopla), vegetables, or greens. But if you are making a potato salad (high starch), then add a leafy green salad and vegetable soup with it. The greens are a must here!

7. **Fats and oils are best used with greens and low starch vegetables:** Never combine high fats with protein. So meats, which are high in saturated fats, will go best with green vegetables or low starch vegetables such as broccoli, cauliflower, carrots, green beans, okra, and red bell peppers. Do not use too much refined oil to cook them. Minimize the use of refined oil with meats.

8. **High-fat proteins like cheese, milk, nuts, yoghurt, and avocado go well with green and non-starchy vegetables, but also with acidic fruits.** Acid slows down the digestion of the protein and also helps with the digestion of the fats present. For example, strawberry with yoghurt and nuts (other acidic/sour fruits are pineapple, kiwi, blueberries), tahini with lime, and meats marinated with good quality vinegars. The digestion of these protein foods which have fat, are greatly aided with the help of green vegetables, as greens benefit the liver where protein is synthesized and used by the body. In case you make a creamy (dairy cream or paneer) salad dressing, add a generous dash of green herbs like parsley, dill, and mint to assimilate better.

DID YOU KNOW?

- Lemons go well with animal protein. Squeezing lemon on some salmon will aid its digestion and balance the yin and yang elements.
- Don't drink water with meals, as drinking dilutes your digestive juices. A small amount of warm water is okay.
- Don't drink fruit juice with the meal. You must for wait two hours or it will upset digestion.

I'm making it very simple for you. Here's a one-week lunch and dinner menu plan, which you can follow. Try it, and see how different you feel a week later.

A ONE-WEEK LUNCH MENU PLAN

	Grain	Bean	Vegetable	Extra
Lunch Menu				
Mon	Whole wheat buns	Curried white beans (chowli)	Curried spinach	Imli and date chutney
Tue	Buckwheat or udon noodles	Khow suey with tofu/beans & veggies	Toppings	Spinach
Wed	Millet with vegetables	Exotic (any yellow lentils with all the whole spices like: cloves, cinnamon, fennel seeds (saunf), cloves, green cardamom pods	Odessa beet salad	Cabbage coleslaw tofu mayo
Thu	Long grain brown rice	Falafel	Thai curry	Spicy red chutney
Fri	Vegetable fried brown rice	Broccoli and tofu in sweet sauce	Sweet corn soup	Kimchi (pressed salad)
Sat	Tortillas	Refried beans	Marinated bell peppers	Endive walnut salad
Sun	Rajgeera roti with spinach	Kaali (Black gram lentils) dal	Fenugreek with carrots	Apple pie (sugarless)

A ONE-WEEK DINNER MENU PLAN

Dinner Menu			
Grain/No grain	**Bean**	**Vegetable**	**Soup**
Rajgeera base pizza	Black bean salad	Vegetable toppings	Red pepper and cauliflower soup (with miso)
Quinoa/ Crackers	Red bean cutlet	Pesto gravy with tofu	Brown rice soup (with miso)
Polenta squares (Polenta is made with corn)	Carribean chowder tofu	Curried spinach	Red pumpkin & leek soup (with miso)
Corn bread/ Makai roti	White beans in tomato sauce	Steam pak choi or spinach	Doodhi soup (with miso)
Chickpea cutlet	Sai bhajee	Nishime-style vegetables	Tomato shorba (with miso)
Sweet potato pancake	Pumpkin seed gravy with tofu	Cucumber and radish salad	Chickpea and cauliflower soup (with miso)
Sweet potato pancake	Mushroom moussaka (eggplant) (without cheese or white sauce)	Boiled veggie salad	Broccoli soup (with miso)

WORKING WITH LEFTOVERS

We've all been put in that spot where we open our fridge to find little bowls of leftovers that you just don't know what to do with. Leftovers can be extremely annoying, since most of us don't have the heart to throw away food. Here are a few ideas for what you can do with leftovers.

1. You can carry over one dish for two meals, so cook enough if you are busy or working.
2. If you make vegetable stock, save the vegetables for a soup the same day or the next.
3. Leftover vegetables can be used in soups (in clear stock) or can be blended to make a nice purée for a gravy dish.
4. Leftover grain can be used to make cutlets, used in a soup to thicken it, as a snack of rice balls, layer it in a baked dish, toss it in a salad, or stir fry it.
5. Leftover legumes can be made into a paste for crackers or bread. Blend it to make a nice gravy, mix it with bread crumbs and some freshly boiled vegetables to make cutlets.
6. If you make nut milk (like the Almond Milk recipe), use the leftover almonds in rotis or your idlis.

SNACKEROOS—TO A HEALTHIER YOU

In India, or anywhere in the world, snack time is essentially junk food time. Every community has its own repertoire and a wide variety of junk food. While most communities do a pretty good job of putting it together, what these snacks generally lack in is nutrition. For example, a dhokla is a great snack, but once you add the baking soda and eno (both to make sure the dough rises), you negate the nutritional value of the snack. A chivda (of any kind) is a great snack, but once you over bake or over roast it and cook it in refined oil (dab it with a tissue paper and see what happens), you again negate the nutritional benefit of this snack. I am not saying don't eat your bhel, but only one in ten times. For the remaining nine, choose a healthier option.

As a health counsellor, chef, and a food consultant, let me tell you this—planning is the name of the snack game. You must have a plan for the week (or have someone do it for you) as to what you like in a snack and how you are going to get it. There are different elements to a snack that make it interesting and unique to every individual. For example, when I was in my twenties, I liked my cinnamon buns and a cup of coffee at 3 pm (of course this was also an indication of my hypoglycemia of which I wasn't remotely aware). Then at around 5 pm I liked a bowl of nice crunchy chivda (the brain likes the crunch sound as it wakes it up; so if you are working at this time, you will crave a crunchy snack). I realized I liked to have something sweet and gooey at 3 pm and then a salted and crunchy snack at 5 pm. This is where the planning begins. Observe your hunger patterns; what do you crave for and at what time of the day. If you can figure these two things out, half the job is taken care of. Now all you have to do is have that snack handy when hunger strikes.

If you are working and live by yourself, then you must have the ability to make the snack and refrigerate it, so you can carry it to work. Although many would argue that freezing kills the nutritional value of food, I'd say that it's much better to have something homemade than something processed from outside.

ESHA DEOL'S SWITCH TO HEALTHY EATING AND SNACKING

Take Esha Deol for example. Esha came to me to get on a healthy diet plan. She loved her snacks. But to be healthy, she knew she couldn't reach out for that packet of nachos or something equally damaging.

We started by replacing her snacks with healthier options. We could not do the meals with her immediately, but she started with fillers for in-between meals. I made her a lot of salad dressings, spreads for bread, and she followed the approach at home. She was committed to the plan. She felt much better, lost some of her weight, and realized the value of eating healthy 24×7. I made sure that I never gave her a chance to fail. Whatever she asked for or craved, we provided. I do that as a rule with all my clients. Her diet was simple—she followed a vegetarian approach and kept her meals centred around grain, vegetables, beans, and good quality fermented foods. This is what she has to say about her new style of eating:

ESHA DEOL'S STORY

'Food, fitness, and a good lifestyle'—this is the general mantra for my generation. Even before the start of my home production, *Tell me o Kkhuda*, Shonali had helped me keep a regular and healthy check on my diet. I simply stuck to my regular workouts at the gym and followed the approach prescribed by her. In fact, there were times when I had to cut down on my workouts for a few months due to my shooting schedules. It was at this time that I realized how easy it was for me to maintain my toned look, despite not working out and learnt that food accounts for 80 percent of a healthy body.

I found that healthy food need not be boring, and that there can be a lot of variety. I could even eat desserts, just as long as they were made with the right natural sweetener. So for six days a week I stuck to this wonderful approach, which took me to another level as far as learning about 'being truly well' goes.

There were times when my skin would break out or I'd have other irregularities like water retention. Shonali worked with food and other simple home remedies to improve my condition. I have never felt hungry, starved, or craved for foods while following this approach. I wanted to find a way to snack healthy, and Shonali always had many delicious snacks at hand for round-the-clock munching.

KEYS TO HEALTHY SNACK PLANNING:

1. *Sunday planning*
Take out your Sunday mornings to figure out a snack menu for the coming week. Make a list of what you'd like to eat and stick it on your refrigerator.

2. *Go shopping*
Make a list of all the ingredients you require for your snacks and hit the stores.

3. Work with leftovers

One of my tricks is to work with leftovers. For example, if you have some extra potatoes left over from the main course, mash them, layer in between bread, and grill. You'll have a sandwich in no time. So cook extra of anything you fancy.

4. Freeze

Organize the snack for each day of the week, put them in zip lock bags, and freeze. Then all you have to do is defreeze it the day you want to eat it.

#See Recipe section for healthy snacking options

PART TWO

9

THE DETOX DIET

Jacqueline and the Beauty Diet detox

It was March 2009. I got a call from someone who introduced herself as Jackie. I assumed it was an expat and without much thought I started her on my meal plan, keeping her special requests in mind. Then one day I received a music CD of the film *Alladin* with a note explaining that Jackie was actually Jacqueline Fernandez, the lead actress of the movie.

Since Jackie started eating my meals, she has never looked back. She loves the food, and is always enthusiastic in her appreciation of anything she likes in particular. On her request I later put her on the detox plan. The first detox diet I scheduled for her was right before her shoot for the Titan ad campaign with Aamir Khan. This is what she had to say about the detox:

'Shonali's detox programme made my bloating vanish. I felt flushed and entirely new! My skin had a natural glow and I felt much lighter. I was calmer, and sailed through the Titan shoot.'

Her detox diet involved simple eating, lots of good fermented foods to clean up her digestive system, more vegetables, miso soup and leafy greens, and a whole grain (in summers, it's usually a lighter grain like millet or quinoa). I kept her off protein till day three, introducing it on a daily basis from day four. And now she's hooked. Every time Jackie has a shoot or has travelled a lot, I put her on a 5-day detox diet and then ensure that she goes back to eating my regular food.

Jackie has been my client for over two years now and this is what she has to say about the approach:

'For me it's the **glow** you feel from within, which can only come about by actually 'eating', not starving yourself, and not fearing carbs. You will never get that glow if you don't eat the right foods. It's like being a child again. I feel, despite all the make up, that natural glow is important for us actresses as it actually symbolizes health and happiness, and that's what's most desirable.'

What is detoxing and why do we need it?

Let's first understand why we need to detox. Detoxing doesn't mean 'to get rid of toxins instantly'. What a detox does is kick start your body, while getting rid of 'some' (not all) of the sludge or toxins that have built up over the years in the blood and the digestive system. Just as you need cleansers and mops to clean your house, similarly you need agents to be introduced into your system to detox or cleanse it. And this can be done through the food you eat. Detoxification basically means cleaning your blood and restoring your body's pH balance to neutral. It does this mainly by removing impurities from the blood, and re-charging all your organs, especially the liver where toxins like old foods sitting there in the form of bad bacteria are processed for elimination from the large intenstines. It also promotes elimination of toxins through the intestines, kidneys, and skin, improves blood circulation, and helps better absorption of nutrients that will benefit you.

Every symptom your body throws up is its way of telling you that something's wrong with it. If you ignore these symptoms and make a beeline for the doctor instead, suppressing them with medication, you can be sure that other symptoms will emerge sooner or later. Anything ranging from bad skin, hair fall, irritable bowel disorder, migraines, being extremely thin or overweight, or chronic fatigue are signs that your body is not in a balanced state. Even emotional outbursts are a sign of the body's blood condition being toxic. If you're always suffering from sinuses, colds, or allergies, it means your body is expelling toxins accumulated from eating fatty foods, sugar, excessive dairy, or processed foods. Your symptoms stem from imbalances created within the body, and 'only' by you. Using antibiotics to control them will only suppress them temporarily, causing more harm to your system.

The body has its own internal mechanism to come back to normal, and that's why it tolerates binges and your extravagant lifestyle. However, if you do it over a number of years without any changes in your lifestyle, your body loses its capacity to bounce back quickly. The system of elimination and filtration (basically bowels, liver, and kidneys) will get overloaded and stop functioning efficiently.

A detox is essential for restoring your body's balance. It's a way of de cluttering the mind and body.

So, it's good to detox to clear up the system, and then start a sound eating plan. Detoxing will strengthen the blood condition and reduce the sludge in it, cleaning your intestines, bringing about a steadiness in your moods, and releasing any stress you might be holding on to, and really rev up your system.

This isn't a raw food or fruits or juices only diet. Be wary of such 'detoxes' because they will leave you feeling extremely weak and cause your blood sugars to go into a tizzy. In my approach, I use foods which will help your body to eliminate the toxins, while providing you with energy so that the body makes a smooth transition to a healthier eating plan. Once you cleanse your body, your own energy (or 'qui', 'prana', or what we call life force that gets clogged when your body gets bogged down with the wrong foods) becomes lighter, and you are ready for new energies to come in. It will free you up emotionally, and make you connect to things and people around you.

When and how often is it recommended?

I recommend a detox when you need to start a new diet plan or when travelling has played havoc with your eating habits and you need to get back to normal. If neither of the above applies to you, then you need to detox once in every four months (the 3-day plan only). If you really need to kick start your body because you have had unhealthy eating habits in the past, then I recommend a 7-day detox programme.

A note before beginning the detox diet

When you begin the detox diet, you may experience a 'discharge', which could be in the form of a headache, stirred up emotions, irritable bowel situation, fatigue, or a cold. But this will only last for a few days and then disappear. However, if these symptoms last longer, then stop the detox and go back to a normal eating plan and once you are stronger, you can start the detox again.

BEFORE YOU START:

1) Eliminate

- Coffee and Indian tea
- Cigarettes
- Sugar, jaggery, honey, artificial sweeteners
- All dairy, animal foods (meat and chicken)
- Anything from a box or processed foods
- Alcohol

- Refined flour (maida)
- Bread and other products that have yeast

2) Include

Make sure you take an extra dose of Vitamin C as this helps the body produce glutathione, a liver compound that drives away toxins.

3) Timing is important.

I recommend a detox when you have time off from work and when you can also relax. Don't start the detox if you are in the middle of a hectic work schedule. Ask yourself this question: is it really a good time for you to start the detox?

4) Don't try to be perfect,

instead be kind to yourself. Know that you will need inner strength and patience. Don't get manic about it.

THE 3-DAY DETOX DIET

The 3-day detox diet is a little more stringent than the 7-day detox diet. This is only because it's a quick cleanse while the other is a longer cleansing process. However, I am mindful of the fact that your body will need nourishment for seven days while it is cleansing. You have to be prepared for this diet. So plan ahead, go shopping, and stock up. These foods will do the job of cleaning the villi (tiny, finger-like projections that protrude from the epithelial lining of the intestinal wall) in your digestive system. This will in turn make room for fresh nutrients. So make sure you have the following before you start the detox (see Recipe section):

- Quick pickles
- Sauerkraut
- Miso paste (if possible)
- Pressed salad

DAY 1

Breakfast
- Lemon, ginger, or tulsi tea, or use the shiitake mushroom tea (see Recipe section)
- A bowl of miso soup (clear made with vegetable stock) and any three vegetables of your choice. If you don't have miso, then any vegetables soup

Lunch
- Pressed salad tossed with green apples (if available) and made with at least three vegetables

Mid-afternoon to evening snack
- Any fruit (one small bowl)

Dinner
- Soup (with miso)
- Boiled vegetables
- Side order of pickles or sauerkraut

DAY 2

Breakfast
- Lemon, ginger, or tulsi tea, or use the shiitake mushroom tea; round vegetable soup with miso

Lunch
- Boiled salad (any three vegetables, for example, cauliflower, green beans, and carrots) tossed with sauerkraut.

Mid-afternoon to evening snack
- Any fruit (one small bowl)

Dinner
- Soup (with miso)
- Steamed vegetables
- Side order of pressed salad

DAY 3

Breakfast
- Lemon, ginger, or tulsi tea, or use the shiitake mushroom tea
- Bowl of millet poha with vegetables

Lunch
- Stir fry vegetables in ½ tsp of oil with a side order of pressed salad

Mid-afternoon to evening snack
- Any fruit (one small bowl)

Dinner
- Soup (with miso)
- Boiled vegetable salad
- Yellow moong dal (no tempering) with salt and pepper
- Side order of pressed salad pickles or sauerkraut

The 7-day detox diet for a good cleanse

DAY 1

Breakfast
- Foxtail millet (cheena) poha or brown rice porridge
- Lemon and ginger tea

Lunch
- Pressed salad
- Sauerkraut
- Plain brown rice with gomashio
- Water sauté of leafy greens (Instead of oil, sauté greens in water)

Mid afternoon
- Sweet vegetable drink
- Fruit (but no banana)

Dinner
- Miso soup
- Boiled salad—any three vegetables. Squeeze some lime on it or make a salad dressing with olive oil, lime, salt, and pepper

- 1 tbs of a quick pickle
- Split lentils if required (no tempering [tarka])

For an in-between meal, snack on pumpkin seeds (unsalted), sesame seeds, or fruit. No juices.

DAY 2

Breakfast
- Clear miso soup (made with vegetable stock); add some greens to it
- Lemon and ginger tea

Lunch
- Nishime-style vegetables
- Sauerkraut
- Small side of chopped white radish and carrots (raw)
- Brown rice with gomashio

Mid afternoon
- Sweet vegetable drink
- Fruit (but no banana) or pumpkin/sunflower seeds

Dinner
- Miso soup
- Blanched salad—any three vegetables with dressing
- Steamed leafy greens
- Quick pickle

DAY 3

Breakfast
- Brown rice poha or millet poha(no oil in poha)
- Lemon and ginger tea

Lunch
- Steamed vegetables (choose any three different coloured ones)
- Pressed salad
- Green smoothie
- Brown rice or foxtail millet (cheena) with gomashio

Mid afternoon
- Sweet vegetable drink
- Fruit (but no banana) or pumpkin/sunflower seeds

Dinner
- Miso soup
- Brown rice (60 percent) and barley (40 percent) cooked with gomashio
- Steamed leafy greens

DAY 4

Breakfast
- Miso soup
- Lemon and ginger tea

Lunch
- Blanched vegetables (choose any three different coloured ones) with salad dressing

- Steamed leafy greens
- Sauerkraut

Snack
- Fruit (but no banana) or pumpkin/sunflower seeds

Mid afternoon
- Sweet vegetable drink

Dinner
- Miso soup
- Brown rice (60 percent) and barley (40 percent) cooked
- Split lentil with tempering (tarka with cumin/mustard seeds)

Day 5

Breakfast
- Brown rice porridge
- Lemon and ginger tea

Lunch
- Miso soup
- Brown rice (40 percent) and barley (20 percent) cooked with gomashio
- Quick pickle
- Blanched leafy greens

Mid afternoon
- Sweet vegetable drink

- Fruit (but no banana) or pumpkin/sunflower seeds

Dinner
- Nishime vegetables
- Steamed leafy greens
- Sauerkraut
- Split lentils with tempering

DAY 6

Breakfast
- Miso clear soup; add leafy green
- Lemon and ginger tea

Lunch
- Pressed salad
- Nishime vegetables
- Steamed leafy greens
- Brown rice with gomashio

Mid afternoon
- Sweet vegetable drink
- Green smoothie

Dinner
- Steamed vegetables
- Sauerkraut
- Miso soup clear

DAY 7

Breakfast
- Brown rice porridge or poha (no oil)
- Green tea or lemon ginger tea

Lunch
- Nishime vegetables
- Pressed salad
- Boiled vegetables
- Blanched vegetables and leafy greens
- Small bowl of brown rice with gomashio

Mid afternoon
- Sweet vegetable drink
- Green smoothie or fruit

Dinner
- Boiled vegetables
- Steamed leafy greens
- Sauerkraut
- Clear miso soup

Note: If you don't have miso handy, just make a regular soup with three vegetables—one of which is a green vegetable.

In a detox diet, the more varied cooking styles are, the better it is.

Body scrubs and how to do it

Your skin is connected to your capillaries and main arteries and veins, and through them to your circulatory system. It discharges toxins all the time, and certain foods such as saturated fats from dairy, meats, and eggs clog up your skin, preventing the passage and elimination of both moisture and oil through your pores. Hence, excess fat which is trying to discharge itself is sent back into your circulatory system through the blood vessels. If this is allowed to continue, over a period of time the circulatory system will get sluggish.

Body scrubs help to activate blood circulation and promote physical and mental energy in the body. They exfoliate your skin, sloughing off dead skin cells and rubbing away hard and flaky skin, leaving it feeling soft and smooth. A scrub can be really invigorating, as it improves the circulation of blood and lymph to the surface of the skin, helping to fight cellulite and improve your skin tone.

Fat will always gather under the skin before it can be discharged. A body scrub draws out the fat and toxins that have collected beneath the surface of the skin. The benefits are visible in many ways: you may feel lighter, sleep better, and feel an improvement in your muscle tone.

For a perfect body scrub, take a small tub filled with hot water—as hot as you can bear. You can even do it under the shower. Take a washcloth (or a face towel). Dip or wet the cloth in the hot water; the cloth should be damp, so squeeze any excess water out of it. Rub it on your skin vigorously, wetting the cloth every now and then as you move to a different part. You can do this before you finish your regular shower or after.

Note: Do not use a coir or plastic loofah to scrub your body, as it is abrasive.

10 tips for your detox

1. Keep yourself hydrated by drinking a lot of water, herbal tea infusions, and green smoothies. Avoid fruit juices unless you feel low on energy in which case make a purée of apples, but warm it before consuming.
2. If you get hungry between meals, eat steamed veggies, fruits, or pumpkin seeds, or make yourself the sweet vegetable drink.
3. Reduce the use of spices and liquid fats (oil) during these seven days.
4. Do not take any protein till after day three. If you crave sweets in the first three days, add protein, preferably fish, to your meals.
5. Include fat dissolving vegetables like white radish, green onions, and cabbage and keep the emphasis on greens.
6. Concentrate on what you're eating and make sure you chew everything well.
7. Include quick pickles, sauerkraut, pressed salads, and miso at all mealtimes.
8. Exercise and do a body scrub daily.
9. Use a ginger compress (see p 240) daily on your stomach area every other day to stimulate the intestine.

10. This should be a quiet and relaxing time for you. So meditate, be calm, and try and keep your BlackBerry far away from you.

The essential pH balance

We live and die on a cellular level. If our cells are healthy, we are healthy and if our cells are unhealthy due to a toxic environment, we are definitely not going to be healthy. Remember yin and yang and how opposites must always be in balance? This also applies to the internal environment of your body.

pH (potential of hydrogen) is a measure of the acidity or alkalinity of a solution. It is measured on a scale of 0 to 14—the lower the pH, the more acidic the solution, the higher the pH, the more alkaline (or base) the solution. When a solution is neither acid nor alkaline, it has a pH of 7 which is neutral. The human body contains about ten gallons of fluid so its cells are swimming in an ocean that is acidic, neutral, or alkaline. At any given time, the blood condition can swing between acidic and alkaline. The body's systems work best in an environment which is neutral or slightly alkaline.

YOUR pH BALANCE IS LOST IF

1. your tongue has a white coating, especially when you wake up in the morning.
2. you suffer from allergies, headaches, low energy, mood swings, skin issues, low libido, insomnia, loss of hair, no vitality, or an ailment for a long span of time.

3. your pH via a blood, urine, or saliva test throws up an acidic result.

TEST YOUR pH

1. Before brushing your teeth, spit into a glass of filtered water. Remember: do not kiss your husband or partner and do not eat or drink anything before you do this.

2. Now wait for ten minutes and watch what happens to the saliva.

If you have a good pH balance, the saliva will be clear and float for a while, then dissolve slowly to the bottom without sinking.

If your body's pH balance is off, the saliva will leave a string-like substance from the top to the bottom of the glass or will be a cloudy mass that will sink to the bottom in whole or in parts.

How is this connected to beauty?

Remember, all your issues with beauty stem from the pH balance being off and excessive candida in your system; which is the case 90 percent of the time. If the acidic load in your body is high, the body will rob you of the alkalinity, especially all your minerals—calcium, magnesium, chromium, iron, potassium, and zinc—which are responsible for keeping your meridian lines unblocked and flushed, resulting in healthy bones, hair, and nails.

The good news is that we can control the body's pH balance by the food we eat. All foods leave behind a residue which is either alkaline or acidic depending on the minerals they contain. However, looking at foods in isolation does not help, as the way they get processed in the body sometimes produces a different condition. For example, milk is alkaline in nature, but when ingested and broken down in the body, it leaves an acidic residue. What you need to do is keep your blood condition on the alkaline side of the pH spectrum. This will keep you beautiful 24x7 and keep your weight down. And the best way to do this is to eat all your good quality fermented foods, because nothing cleans the stomach villi and restores your body pH faster.

Below is a list of foods that are alkaline, acidic, and neutral; just remember, if you can eat 80 percent alkaline foods and 20 percent acid-forming foods, you are doing well. Also, refer to the food combinations explained in Part I (see p 148), which will help you to understand how you should eat to aid the breakdown of these foods. Just remember the cleaner your digestive system, the more energy you will have. It will also help slow down the ageing process, bring back the glow in your skin, and keep your weight stable.

pH BALANCE TRANSITIONING POINTERS

1. Eat your veggies.
2. Include avocados, lime, tomatoes, pomegranate, and sprouts in your diet.
3. Include a green smoothie on a daily basis.
4. Include a daily probiotic supplement (available from your local chemist in sachets or ampoules) and fermented foods at each meal.

DON'T

1. have sugar in any form.
2. eat fruit (till the body has restored its pH balance).
3. have any processed foods, simple carbohydrate, dairy, meats, refined oil, eggs, yeast or yeasted products, coffee, or alcohol.

#Beauty Tip: Lime juice has an instant alkaline affect. So if you are sick, squeeze a lime in a glass, add the same amount of water to make a lime shot, and drink it up.

10

THE FACE DIET

Beauty is skin deep

My friend Tina Grewal, a beauty aesthetician who gives me the best facials, has always maintained that I have great skin. I have been going to her for fifteen years now, and she tells me that my skin has not aged or changed at all. She says it feels like my collagen has regenerated over time and has stayed the same. I'm not blowing my own trumpet, but I am often asked what foundation I use, when in fact I use none. So I assume this means that I have good skin. During one of my facial sessions the subject of good skin came up. And I told her that my skin is the way it is because of my diet over the years. Also being a non smoker and not much of a drinker helps. Here, my dear friend completely baffled me. She protested against my philosophy. She insisted that one's diet had very little to do with skin. So I kept my cool and tried and reason with her; 'Well what do *you* think is at play when women come to you with really bad skin?'

'Hormones,' came her quick reply.

'What, do you think, affects hormones?'

'Tch, Shonali, hormones are hormones and they can act up anytime. Food has nothing to do with it.'

I tried one last time. 'Hormones are chemical messengers that go directly into your bloodstream. If your blood condition is sludgy and congested with mucous, how the hell are the hormones going to reach their target area? This in itself causes a 'hormonal imbalance'. And what is your blood condition affected by, if not the food you eat every day?'

Priya Batra, a highly motivated and dedicated investment banker, is slim, tall, and has light eyes, but her skin was riddled with acne and she had perennial dark circles. All her beauty was under a cloud. When she came to me, she suffered from constipation and low energy levels. It was clear to me that her fatigue and acne was a result of her weak digestive system.

Her diet revealed that she had been quite deficient in her eating habits: a lot of raw food, no adequate protein, lots of nuts and dates throughout the day, which is the worst thing to eat because it dries out your digestive tract when you are constipated.

I focused on solving her constipation as I knew the skin would respond eventually once she started changing her diet. I made her stick to a basic diet of grains, beans, vegetables, good fermented foods (sauerkraut, pressed salads, and pickles), and fruit. I took out all the processed stuff and dairy, added spirulina to her diet, a veggie smoothie daily, the nishime cooking style (two to three times per week) and a sweet vegetable drink daily. I minimized her intake of nuts and dates (way too much concentrated sugar for her, but it indicated that her body wanted quick bursts of energy, as her adrenal glands were being pushed because of constant constipation). Digestion takes up 80 percent of your total energy, and if you are not eating the right foods or your digestive system is not functioning well, it will damage your system.

Six weeks after she met me, her constipation had improved by 80 percent. But what was amazing was that her skin had cleared up, and the dark bags under the eyes were ten shades lighter (indicative of her kidneys [adrenals] functioning better due to a cleaner digestive system).

However, Priya slipped with her diet, and her symptoms returned, so I worked with her again, helping her get back on track. Her skin started showing the change in her blood condition and was glowing. Her acne was a thing of the past. She had higher energy levels and was happier and less anxious than when I met her for the first time. Nupur now knows what works for her and what doesn't; she strives daily to maintain her diet and keeps at it.

Just remember: your intestines are connected to all your nerve pathways, meridian lines (nadis), and also connected through these pathways to every organ in your body. A back up of toxicity due to constipation or sluggish elimination will cause all parts of your body to be severely affected. If our digestive system is clear, not only will energy flow freely, but each organ will be affected and this will reflect first on your skin. Also y*our colon is a reflection of your mind,* so a clean colon leads to a calmer and radiant mind!

There's such a fuss about glowing skin. We all want it. Most of my clients ask me how they can get that 'glow'. Turn on the TV and half the advertisements are for products which will give us not only better but 'glowing' skin. Flip through a glossy magazine, and you're bound to get tips on keeping your skin healthy. Skin care is vital because skin covers the outer body, which makes it most vulnerable to dust, pollution, seasonal changes, etc. Mental and physical stress directly affects the skin. Ever wondered why your skin breaks out before your periods or if you have a bad stomach? It is because the skin is a mirror of how our organs are functioning in the body and our state of mind. If our insides aren't happy, it's bound to show on the skin. You need to know what's going on inside to fix the outer problems.

DID YOU KNOW?

Skin forms the largest organ of the body, comprising of almost 20 square feet (in most adults) and accounting for about 16 per cent of a person's weight. Each 5 square cm of skin may have up to 600 sweat glands, 20 blood vessels, 60,000 melanocytes, and over a thousand nerve endings. Among many functions of the skin is protection, sensation, heat regulation, excretion of sweat, and water resistance (to keep essential nutrients from washing out of the body).

Your face and meridian lines: the mirror to your insides

You've been staring into the mirror and you've just spotted the first dark spot on your cheekbone. It wasn't there before. 'Or was it?' You wonder. Wait a minute, there's another one. You peer closely, your nose now pressed against the mirror, and you panic, because you've always had relatively spotless skin, except for that pimple that obediently appears before your period. Is this what ageing is? Are you growing old? The panic soon reaches a crescendo and you find yourself in a mall at a luxurious body products store stacking up on everything that has an 'anti-ageing' label on it.

Stop. Here's your body trying to tell you something. Your face reveals a lot more about you than just your genetics. Hidden behind your facial elements is the history of your body, blood condition, and what ails it. So says Traditional Chinese Medicine on which the macrobiotic diet is based. This ancient belief system emphasizes that in the embryonic stage, when the body is being formed, the imprint of the organs is reflected on the face. The constitution of the body is also determined by the health of the sperm and egg during conception. Hence our posture, colour of skin, tone of voice, and other traits are mere external manifestations of our blood, organs, nervous system, and skeletal structure. During the embryonic stage, all major systems of the body, namely the digestive and respiratory, the nervous, and the circulatory and excretory systems, gather and form your facial structure, sharing four major areas of your face. According to this principle, each area of the face represents a particular organ and its corresponding functions. Even the way your mother ate during her pregnancy is written all over you. For example, eyelids that are swollen and red or purple indicate excessive intake of fruits, sugar and other sweets, soda, soft drinks, alcohol, and stimulants consumed during pregnancy.

I spend a lot of time with each of my clients, and since I only do one consultation a day, I give each client enough time. My diagnosis starts the moment a client walks in. And since your body and face is a reflection of your internal systems, I can immediately tell what's going on inside you.

The next step is to diagnose the health of your organs via the meridian lines (Chinese system) or nadis (Indian system). The basic assumption of Eastern philosophies is that all life contains energy known as prana in Sanskrit, or chi in Chinese. And the health of any organism is a fine interplay of this energy, Shiva and Shakti, yin and yang, or the mind and the body. When these energies are balanced, the body will be healthy. Within the human body, these energies flow along a network of channels or lines (nadis or meridians). In the Yoga tradition, there are said to be 72,000 nadis. Each has a specific function and energy that it deals with.

Every organ has its own meridian line, and these meridian lines get blocked with bad foods, lifestyle, and disease. My job as a health counsellor is to get to the root of the problem, which is to interpret the cause of the blockage, and remedy it with food and lifestyle adjustments. For example, the webbing between your thumb and index finger has a meridian line (LI4) which connects to the large intestine meridian. If I press it correctly and you feel pain, it is an indication that there is something wrong in your stomach. Also its texture will give me an indication of the muscle tone in your intestines. There's very little you can hide from me!

Once I know where to look and how the organs are functioning, I can make sound recommendations based on what's causing the imbalances within your body, so that you start looking good. So go get a mirror and start your own facial diagnoses. The macrobiotic approach to look beautiful in every way is based on how you function as a whole, and is unlike modern approaches which use tools to take away your problem from the surface alone. My job is to see how your organs are pulling together and giving you that gorgeous face, great hair, a fabulous body, and vitality.

Go ahead and diagnose yourself

THE FACE

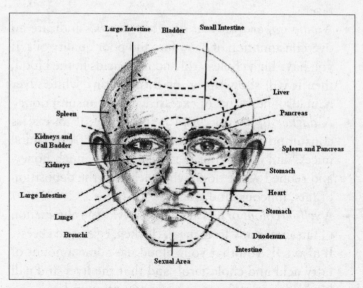

Photo credit: *Your Body Never Lies* by Michio Kushi

THE FOREHEAD

The upper forehead represents the circulatory and excretory systems, that is the heart, kidneys, and bladder. If the upper forehead area is clean with no irregular skin colour, it is indicative of a sound kidney, heart, and bladder function. However, if this area shows any of the above mentioned problems, then you have to address your eating patterns.

- A *red colour* in this region means that your circulatory system is pushed due to the over consumption of liquids, juices, fruits, other drinks, alcohol, or coffee, pushing the excretory system into overdrive, causing frequent urination, indigestion, and diarrhoea. You could also be suffering from a faster pulse rate and fever.

- A *pale upper forehead* or *white patches* indicate an overconsumption of dairy fats and poor quality oils. If you have high cholesterol and fatty acids in the blood, then it will show up in the form of tiny white/silver hair, also indicative of excessive dairy consumption.

- A *darker upper forehead* is indicative of an excess consumption of sugar, including sugar from fruits, juices, and milk. Your diet includes too much honey, and refined white flour, which leads to the deposition of fats, mucous, and stones.

- A *yellow colour or patches* is indicative of an elimination of fats, especially from meat, chicken, eggs, and cheese. It also tells you that your blood has some amount of fatty acid and cholesterol, and that the liver and gall bladder are not functioning at an optimum level.

- *Pimples* in this region indicate excessive consumption of various foods. R*ed pimples* indicate excessive consumption of fruits, sugars, juices, coffee, and stimulating liquids. *White pimples* indicate excessive consumption of fats, and oils. Yellow *pimples* indicate excessive consumption of animal fats and cholesterol. D*ark pimples* indicate excessive consumption of dense protein (like animal foods). *Moles* and *warts* are also reflective of this.

The middle forehead corresponds to the nervous system and good intellectual capacity.

- *A red colour* shows an excessive consumption of stimulants, soft drinks, fruits, juices, and other beverages, and is generally accompanied by anxiety, nervousness, and emotional upheaval.
- *A white colour* while indicative of excessive dairy consumption, also belies dullness and clouded mental activity.
- *A yellow colour* shows an excessive intake of eggs, chicken, and dairy foods. Such a person will also be inflexible and not willing to change.
- *Red pimples* show the elimination of sugar, excessive fruits, and white flour products.
- *Freckles* in this region are usually due to an elimination of excessive sugars, fruits, honey, juices, milk sugars and other sweets or chemicals, drugs, and excessive medication.

The lower forehead corresponds to the digestive and respiratory systems.

- A *red colour* in this region is indicative of over consumption of fat from animal foods, vegetable oils, fruits (and fruit juices or excessive vegetable juices), sugar, alcohol, and other liquids.
- *White patches, pimples,* and *spots* indicate that your diet has caused an accumulation of fats and mucous mainly in your lungs and digestive system by the excessive consumption of eggs, chicken, and dairy products.
- *Red pimples* are indicative of excessive juices, fruits, sugars, anitibiotics, and foods with chemicals.
- *White pimples* are caused due to excessive fats.
- *Yellowish pimples* are caused due to an excessive consumption of animal foods and cholesterol; *dark pimples* are due to undigested protein and fat—usually from meat.
- A *dark colour* is telling of your respiratory and digestive function slowing down due to the consumption of excessive salt, baked products, meat, eggs, and dried foods. This may be accompanied by constipation and breathing issues.
- A *green colour* shows an accumulation of fat and mucous leading to cysts, tumours, or even cancer in the respiratory and digestive systems. This is usually due to an overconsumption of animal fat, foods, and drinks with sugar, dairy, fruits, medication, drugs, or refined flour.

IN BETWEEN THE EYEBROWS

This region represents the liver and gall bladder.

- *Vertical lines* are a sign that there is an accumulation of fats and mucous in the liver. The more the lines, the harder and slower in purifying blood is the liver.
- *Small lines* are a response to greasy foods. Once you move on to the correct diet, the lines will slowly lessen.
- *Yellow patches, together with vertical lines* indicate the development of stones and cysts in the liver.
- *Puffiness* is indicative of excessive sweet consumption.

The bridge of the nose corresponds to the health of the pancreas.

- *Lines* show that the pancreas is being pushed to its maximum due to the excessive consumption of eggs, sugars, simple sugars (white carbs).
- *White or yellow patches* show that the liver is fatty.
- *Pimples* indicate that the liver may be reacting to animal foods and eggs.
- *Flaky, dry skin* shows that your diet is high in fats and lacks vegetables.

The temples correspond to the function of the spleen, pancreas, liver, and gall bladder.

- A *dark colour* shows sugar elimination, which includes cane sugar, jaggery, honey, juices, chocolates, and dairy as well as food on the other extreme like salty and dried foods. If the texture of the skin is not smooth, it indicates a sluggish pancreas, liver, spleen, and kidneys.

- *Pimples* are indicative of these organs eliminating extreme foods like sugars, meat, salt, and refined flour products.

EYES

We spend so much time on under-eye creams, anti-wrinkle creams, and other cosmetics which promise to bring the sparkle back to the eyes. We don't realize that the eyes represent the entire physical, mental, and spiritual condition of a person. Shape, distance between eyes, angle of the eyes, their size, and eyelids represent a lot of things. The colour, skin, and condition of skin around the eyes relates to how you are eating and eliminating. A clean, smooth, and natural skin tone is reflective of sound mental health and the result of a good diet and lifestyle.

- A *dark colour around the eyes* reflects contraction in the kidneys due to exhaustion, and an elimination of hard-baked products (like bread consumption daily), intake of excessive salt, roasted, baked, and dried foods.
- A *reddish skin colour around the eyes* is usually because the blood capillaries are expanded due to the consumption of sweets, sugars from liquids like alcohol, soft drinks, and fruits, indicating that the heart and circulatory systems are not functioning well, and that there is stagnation in the kidneys.
- A *purplish colour* around the eyes usually occurs due

to the consumption of drugs, sugars, medications, chemicals, and sugary drinks.

- A *yellow colour around the eyes* shows that the liver and gall bladder are being over worked, usually due to the consumption of excessive cheese and dairy.

- A *greyish colour* indicates that the kidneys are not functioning well; and also that the lungs may be stagnated due to excessive intake of animal food, salt, and eggs. This colour also shows that the endocrine (hormonal) system, especially the reproductive organs, are not balanced.

- *Pimples around the eyes* shows that the body is trying to eliminate fats and protein (usually animal); *red pimples* are due to excessive sugars, while *yellow pimples* indicate an excessive intake of animal food as a result of which the spleen, pancreas, and kidneys are being pushed to their limits.

- *Pimples below the lower eyelid* indicate that the body is eliminating fats, protein, and sugar caused by an excessive consumption of fatty meats and sugars or fruits and fruit juices and dairy.

- *Pimples on the eyelid* are indicative of eliminations of fats and proteins and sugars. If you eat too much fruit, juices, and citrus fruits, you may get pimples at the corners of your eyelids.

- The *area above the eyes, under the eyebrows*, tends to sag and wrinkle, or become puffy and loose due to bad eating habits. Many women prefer to get a botox treatment to cure the problem when in reality, eating a balanced diet will stop the skin from sagging, and keep it supple, smooth, and youthful.

- The most common condition which people blame lack of sleep for is *puffiness around the eyes*, which is actually due to the overconsumption of liquids. When the kidneys and liver are being pushed to their limits, or there is a severe case of mucous around your kidneys, it is usually manifested in this form. If these eyebags (watery and swollen) are due to excessive liquid intake, it will be accompanied with frequent urination and lack of sleep indicating that the kidney function is affected.
- The *eyebags which appear swollen and fatty* are due to a mucous build up.
- If you have *pimples or dark spots on the mucous caused eyebags,* it is indicative that there is mucous and fat in the kidneys, leading to stones. Eyebags are usually an important sign that the overall energy of the body will be affected, as the kidneys are the powerhouse for energy. This in turn will affect your vitality.
- *Wrinkled skin under the eyes* indicate that the kidneys are tired and really pushed as a result of too much salt and animal protein in the diet.

NOSE

The nose is a reflection of the nervous and circulatory systems, and certain functions of the digestive system. The size, shape, and structure reveal a lot about the character of a person. The sides of the nose show the liver function.

- A *hard-tipped nose* indicates a saturated fat build up in the body, especially from animal foods like meats, chicken, eggs, cheese, and dairy products. This will also result in hardening of arteries in this area, and indicates an accumulation of fat around the heart, liver, kidneys, spleen, and prostate. A lot of men have this condition.

- A *swollen tip* shows excessive intake of sugar, fruits, fluids, and an excess of fats and oils. It also means the circulatory and excretory systems are not in order.

- A *cleft nose* shows an excessive intake of sugars, fruits, fruit or vegetable juices, soft drinks, all of which rob you off minerals and complex sugars.

- An excessively *red nose* with broken capillaries shows excessive liquid intake, alcohol, coffee, stimulants, and spices. People with such a condition usually suffer from blood pressure, and have a tendency towards hypertension.

- If the *entire nose is red*, then the liver is also not functioning well.

- *Expanded, broken capillaries in the skin of the nose* are indicative of the liver and heart being overburdened. Excessive salt consumption will cause the skin on the nose to be *white and pale*, also indicating that the diet has almost no vegetables and fluids. The hands and feet of such people are usually cold and they have a sweaty skin.

- *Red pimples* show an elimination of sugars, stimulants, fruits; while *white or yellow pimples* show an elimination of dairy, animal fats, and dairy foods.

CHEEKS

The cheeks represent the respiratory and circulatory systems and outer regions of the digestive system. An imbalance will show up in colour, texture, spots, pimples and small veins on the cheek. Taut, firm, and smooth flesh with a good colour shows a good respiratory and circulatory system.

- *Thin cheek flesh* shows a lack of protein and fat in the diet.
- *Visible veins* indicate nutrition deficiency.
- *White or pale cheeks* indicate excessive dairy product consumption especially cheese, creamy products, yoghurt. This could also happen if one eats too much refined flour. This is also accompanied by a sense of lethargy and sluggishness, as there is accumulation of fat in the large intestine and lungs and the person may also be suffering from anaemia.
- *Red or pink cheeks* show that there is an overconsumption of soft drinks, coffee, alcohol, stimulants, fruits, fruit juices, medication, and drugs.
- *Dark spots* are a sign of fat or mucous accumulation in some parts of the lungs, a lot of coffee, and stimulants can also be the cause of these.
- As for the issue which affects most teenagers and women, *pimples*—they are an indication of an elimination of excessive fats and mucous caused by the intake of chicken, meats, dairy, oils, fats, and a heavy build up of mucous and fats in the lungs, reproductive areas, and digestive system. Most of my clients who suffer from polycystic ovarian syndrome

(PCOS) have this problem. Severe acne and pimples are usually also accompanied by a vaginal discharge or cysts in the reproductive areas.

- *White pimples* indicate excessive dairy and sugar consumption; *yellow pimples* indicate excessive cheese, chicken and eggs.
- Excessive sugar, honey, jaggery, or salt and dried foods will cause the cheeks to have a *dark colour. Freckles* on the cheeks are indicative of an elimination of sugars, jaggery, fruit sugars, and milk sugars, while also indicating that these foods are harming your lungs.
- *Cheek hair* which are very fine, silvery, and small indicate an excessive consumption of dairy, and poorly functioning reproductive and digestive organs.

THE MOUTH

We are all obsessed with our mouth, lips, and what they show of us. Dry, flaky, chapped lips, or those with lines say a lot about your condition. The mouth specifically represents the digestive organs and their functioning. While the structure of the lips, whether full, thin, or small is inherited, the condition in and around the lips is in our hands. Different areas of the mouth represent specific organs and functions. For example, the upper lip shows the condition of the upper part of the digestive system, while the lower lip shows the condition of the lower digestive tract, especially the small and large intestine.

- *Lip colour* has a lot to say about how we eat. A *pinkish-red colour* shows good blood quality and circulation, also indicating that the respiratory, circulatory, and digestive functions are good.

- *Pale lips* indicate a haemoglobin deficiency, anaemia, and a lethargic circulation.
- *Dark lips* indicate that the blood has too many salts and fatty acids, and shows a slowness in the kidneys, bladder, and liver function. *Dark lips with a redness* shows an overconsumption of protein and saturated fats. It also indicates a weakness in the spleen, pancreas, kidneys, and urinary tract.
- *Pinkish-white* lips show an excessive consumption of dairy, sugars, fats, fruits, also indicating hormonal disorders and a weak lymphatic system. People who have allergies, skin issues, or asthma may often have lips of this colour.
- *Yellowish* lips show an excessive consumption of cheese, eggs, and chicken; these foods cause the liver and gall bladder to harden and weaken their ability to properly eliminate this build up.
- *Black spots* show excessive carbohydrate consumption in the form of sugar, honey, jaggery, fruits, and their sugars.
- *White patches* show overconsumption of dairy, eggs, chicken, and especially cheese, interfering with the liver functions due to the build up of these saturated fats.
- *Vertical wrinkles on the lips* show that the hormonal functions are weak, and a decline in the sexual functions. These wrinkles also indicate that your body is dehydrated, or that there is excessive consumption of salt and dried foods.

- A *swollen lower lip* shows an imbalance in the small and large intestine which is indicative of a problem in the stomach. A *swollen upper lip* also indicates stomach disorders. *Crusty skin accumulation at the corner of the mouth* shows excessive use of poor quality oil, greasy foods, and animal protein; if it is yellow in colour, it shows a liver disorder stemming from saturated fats such as meat, chicken, eggs, and cheese.

CHIN

The chin represents the reproductive organs. A *red chin with expanded capillaries* shows an excessive intake of sugars, spices, and stimulants; in men it indicates an inflamed prostate. A chin which is thick in texture, has wrinkles, or looks swollen, in both men and women, is also indicative of the reproductive organs being affected in some way. Pimples on the chin show an elimination from the reproductive organs, indicating an accumulation of fats and mucous in these areas caused by overconsumption of dairy, meats, eggs, chicken, and sugar.

KICK THAT BUTT

Inhaling just one puff of a cigarette generates more than a trillion free radicals in your lungs, which triggers an inflammatory response in all organs, including the epidermis. Tobacco constricts blood vessels, which reduces blood flow to the skin and results in a grey, lifeless, and unhealthy-looking complexion, as well as leathery skin that wrinkles much faster.

Vitamins and the Skin and Where to Get them	
Vitamin A (antioxidant)	Retinol and beta carotene are necessary for smooth and healthy skin. Vitamin A keeps skin elastic and prevents dryness, wrinkling, and ageing by stimulating collagen. A deficiency of this vitamin results in dry skin, itching, roughness, pimples, accumulation of dandruff, and splitting of nails. Food sources: squash (bhopla), carrots, all yellow vegetables, dark leafy greens, broccoli, and spirulina
Vitamin B2	Riboflavin, transports oxygen and is essential to metabolize carbohydrates. A deficiency of this vitamin makes you wrinkle faster and get lines, produces whiteheads, fat deposits on skin, and cracking around the mouth. If you have oily hair, it could be due to this vitamin being deficient. It also helps control the body's acidity levels. Food sources: all whole grains, spirulina, legumes, green vegetables, animal foods—especially liver, carrots, red peppers, eggplant, and tomatoes
Vitamin B3	Niacin, keeps your circulation going, and ensures adequate supply of oxygen to the skin, hair, and nails. Maintains healthy tissue, helps in metabolizing fat and carbohydrate. A deficiency of this vitamin can cause scaling in the skin, dry skin, and skin disorders. Food sources: all whole grains, legumes, fish, leafy greens, brewer's yeast, wheat bran, nuts, and seeds
Vitamin B5	Pantothenic acid, helps convert carbohydrates to energy. It acts like an anti-inflammatory prerequisite for skin disorders and aids in keeping the skin healthy. It is also called the 'anti-stress' vitamin. Food sources: all whole grains, cabbage, all green vegetables, corn, cauliflower, sunflower seeds, unrefined vegetable oils, mushrooms, avocados, and eggs

Vitamin B6	Pyridoxine, helps in metabolizing fat, protein, and carbohydrates. Maintains hormones, skin, and all nerves. A deficiency of this vitamin causes oily, dry, and sometimes scaly skin; its deficiency also tends to cause dandruff. Food sources: whole grains—especially brown rice and buckwheat (kuttu), legumes, cabbage, carrots, fish, sunflower seeds, brewer's yeast, wheat bran, and bananas
Vitamin B9	Folic acid,** helps with the formation of red blood cells and also helps the body synthesize fats. A deficiency of this vitamin can cause anaemia, and greatly reduce nutrition to skin and hair; it will also cause the skin to lose its colour and make it blotchy. If you had hangnails (small, torn pieces of skin at the corners of the nails), it is a sign that you may be deficient in this vitamin and also in Vitamin C and protein. Food sources: whole grains, leafy greens, spirulina, red kidney beans, chickpeas, wheatgerm, avocado, beetroot, raspberries, asparagus
Inositol	Associated with the growth of your hair and often used to reverse hair loss. A deficiency can cause eczema. Combines with choline (a water-soluble nutrient like salt essential for body functions, obtained through foods you eat) to move fats out of your liver. Food sources: oats (whole), barley (jov), whole grains, legumes, and seeds **PABA, or para-aminobenzoic acid, makes up a part of the folic acid molecule and a deficiency can cause premature graying. Good food sources include citrus fruits, beans, nuts, whole grains, and a daily dose of fibre.

Vitamin C (antioxidant)	Ascorbic acid, together with protein, helps build collagen and elastin, both crucial for soft, plump, toned skin. Aids in healing of wounds, bones, and red blood cells formation. Very crucial in strengthening elasticity of your blood vessel walls and healthy cell membranes. A deficiency of this vitamin will reduce the collagen in your skin, cause your skin to hang and get wrinkles, change the colour of the skin, causing early ageing. If you are eating animal food, then it is necessary to take this vitamin as it counteracts the yang effects of animal food; being a 'yin' vitamin. Food sources: All dark leafy greens, broccoli, cabbage, melons, strawberries, apricots, any seasonal fruit—especially guava, melons, papaya; all yellow vegetables like yellow peppers, yellow squash, sprouted seeds, and beans
Vitamin E (antioxidant)	Tocopherol, helps with the oxidation of unsaturated fatty acids, Vitamin C and A, and metabolic processes in the body; aids blood circulation, slows down the ageing process, and keeps skin looking young. Helps in interaction of oxygen with other chemicals in the body. Food sources: all leafy green vegetables, broccoli, whole grains, soybeans and other whole beans, sunflower and sesame seeds, tuna and sardines *TIP: Vitamin E is easily destroyed if you deep fry or add too much heat to the food (for example, baking, broiling), so lightly cook fresh veggies sometimes to get the maximum amount of this vitamin from food*

Two building blocks of your beauty (hair, skin, nails, and vitality), and how to get them

1. MINERALS

Minerals and trace elements are responsible for building tissue and regulating a lot of your body's processes. Most of the essential minerals must be supplied through food, as they are not made by your body. Eating plants (vegetables) is a good source of minerals; the greener the vegetable, the better. But the quality of minerals is largely dependent on the quality of the soil.

Remember, the two most important organs that create energy in your body are the adrenals and thyroid, and they need a constant supply of minerals. If you have low energy, you end up craving simple carbohydrates to boost your energy levels, albeit temporarily. And since you are already low on minerals, your body will leach on the minerals from your teeth, bones, and nails to make up for the imbalance.

Apart from the approach of whole grains, legume/fish, vegetables, and fermented foods, let's look at what minerals we need, why we need them, and what other foods they can be sourced from.

Mineral	Why We Need It?	Extra Food Sources
Zinc	carries carbon dioxide from your cells to your lungs; maintains blood sugar levels; maintains an acid-alkaline balance in the body; helps prevent ageing; builds collagen; prevents wrinkles	Sardines, oysters, wheat germ, pumpkin seeds, sesame seeds and sesame seed butter-tahini, dark chocolate, lamb, liver, egg yolk, spirulina

Iron	transports oxygen and carbon dioxide to and from cells; forms a large part of enzymes in our body; necessary for energy, which translates to ageing; oxygen will keep your blood healthy and result in that glowing skin; gives you restful sleep	Meat, fish, chicken, pumpkin seeds, almonds, dates, tofu, sunflower seeds, cantaloupe, leafy greens, and spirulina
Magnesium	strengthens bones, teeth, and nails; necessary for energy; necessary for keeping your bowels functioning; important for Vitamin D absorption	All green veggies with chlorophyll, spirulina, whole grains, cashews, almonds, avocado, raisins (for more see Part I)
Calcium	strengthens bones, teeth, nails; controls cholesterol; aids the absorption of B12; affects sleep quality; keeps your weight in check	Leafy greens, spirulina, milk (read about milk in Part I), salmon, sardines, sesame seeds, millet, almonds, parsley, pumpkin seeds
Silicon	mineral of youth; gives you lustrous hair and strong nails; healthy skin, maintains muscle elasticity and keeps them flexible; affects your tendons and ligaments (essential if you exercise)	Leafy greens, all plant-based foods, whole grains, nuts, spirulina
Potassium	maintains fluid levels in the body; helps to maintain blood sugar levels, thereby helping with weight issues;	Brewer's yeast, spirulina, dates, avocados, grapes, salmon, baked potatoes, dried peaches, tomato

	encourages good bowel movements; cleanses at a cellular level	juice, paprika, dark chocolate, dried apricots, pumpkin/flax/chia/ sunflower seeds
Chromium	balances blood sugar levels; helps to reduce food cravings; protects DNA and RNA (essential in the ageing process)	Beef, liver, eggs, chicken, apples, bananas, leafy greens, wheat germ, spirulina

2. ENZYMES

You can eat all the healthy food you want, but if you have a history of unhealthy eating patterns and poor digestive health, then chances are you are going to need all the enzymes to break down your food. Enzymes deplete as your system ages and so do the acids necessary for digestion in your stomach. So you need to keep replenishing these. While the fermented foods quotient in the approach takes care of this, let's look at what else can help us get our enzymes and what they can do for us.

Enzymes will help you:

- assimilate the nutrients from your food better.
- lose weight.
- age better as they repair your DNA.
- get that glow on the skin.

As I mentioned earlier, while fermented foods and a plant-based approach will give you the enzymes you need, a sure shot way of getting both minerals and enzymes is through a green smoothie daily (see recipe on p 293). It gives you a dose of enzymes to predigest a meal and your necessary minerals.

BEAUTY JUICES

Juices have the complete goodness of both enzymes and minerals. They are the surest way of getting all the necessary components to make you look beautiful, to give you great teeth, nails, hair, and skin. (See Recipe section for juice recipes).

DOS ABOUT JUICING:

- Start after you have done a detox, and have started following the pH balance principles for at least three months.
- Always use your mixer and not your juicer, and don't separate the pulp of the veggies from the juice; make the juice by adding some water to the veggies.
- Always drink within fifteen minutes of making the juice.
- Chew the pulp before you take it down, do not chug your juice down.
- Drink your juice on an empty stomach.
- Always add some lemon juice into the juice before drinking.
- Add spirulina or wheat grass powder if you have decided to incorporate these into your diet (I encourage this strongly).
- If you are coming out of a candida issue, I also encourage adding a probiotic sachet or liquid formula

to your juice; this will add the friendly bacteria that your healing stomach will need.

> ### Did you know...
>
> Sprouts have upto 30 percent more protein, almost 1000 percent more enzymes and more vitamin and chlorophyll stores, than any other isolated foods. The body requires minimal energy to digest them (as the complex sugars within them are broken down), and one actually gains energy from them, as in the process of growing from a seed to the sprouting stage, it gathers more life force. So incorporate them as much as possible in your daily diet.

Skin care tips

- **Sleep:** Make it a habit to put your BB on silent when you tuck in. Sleep is vital, and it's called the beauty sleep for a reason. Also, try and go to bed at the same time every day. Try this for a week and your body clock will get set.
- **Clean bowels:** If you skip this step in the morning, be sure that it'll show on your face. Those are toxins that you're holding in. You can have triphala to aid this process.
- **Exercise:** Go for a brisk walk, run, or just jump around in your room. There's nothing like a rush of endorphins to give you a quick glow for a night out.
- **Cleanse, tone, and moisturize every morning and before going to bed:** The most popular and effective short-term skincare regime, which yields maximum benefits.

- **Stay happy:** A relaxed mind is the key to everything. And I'm sure you've heard that before.
- **Stay natural:** Try to use natural products if possible or be conscious and minimize the use of chemical products like in your make up, hair colour, deodorants, and any other skin and hair products.
- **Cold water:** Wake up and splash your face with cold water. It helps to get rid of the dead cells.
- Give yourself a **facial** on weekends.

3 SUPPLEMENTS FOR YOUR SKIN:

Green tea extract—acts as an antioxidant, protects against free radicals and cancers, and has anti-inflammatory properties.

Coenzyme Q10—Helps build new skin cells, and minimizes wrinkles.

Mushrooms—especially shiitake, will help build good quality blood; mushrooms are anti-inflammatory in nature.

THE HAIR STORY

My grandmother always told me about what great hair my mother had. A stewardess with Air India in the 1960s, she was known for her bouffant, which she made out of her own hair without any props. Then as age came along, her hair started thinning; she used a lot of products which weren't as chemical free as some of today's stuff, and her diet was also high in sugar and fat. My hairstylist (my friend Dilshad) has always said that my hair—even with the colour in it—has not changed much over the years. I don't accessorize my hair that much. It takes very little to take care of it. Yes, I do oil it about once a week, but my food habits have supported the health of my hair all these years.

In the Ayurvedic theory, your hair are your 'roots' while in the Chinese system of diagnosis, hair symbolizes your vitality. It reflects the functioning of your digestive and reproductive systems. Strong, shining, and a good head of hair indicates that your overall energy, your chi, the life force, is good and you have good health. Our hair is also a reflection of what's going on inside our bodies. Hair is made up of a protein keratin, and this comes from a diet rich in this protein.

Creating a good condition for our hair by choosing the right foods is in our hands. Dry, thinning, brittle, falling hair or dandruff, split ends, and graying hair is the result of our food habits and lifestyle. It has little to do with the environment we live in and marginally to do with what we inherited from our parents.

 You can supplement the health of your hair with Vitamin C, B vitamins, Omega 3, Vitamin D, A, and E.

7 TIPS FROM CELEBRITY HAIRSTYLIST DILSHAD PASTAKIA ON HOW TO GET HEALTHY HAIR:

1. Trim your hair every six weeks to maintain your hairstyle, and once in three months for growing it longer.

2. Massage hair with 1 tbs of castor+olive oil or coconut oil for twenty minutes and wash it off in an hour.

3. For dry hair, mix a cup of fresh mayo+olive oil+2 eggs (eggs are excellent for prevention of hair fall) +1 banana. Mash it all together and apply from top to ends. Leave it on only for fifteen minutes or max thirty minutes and rinse with cold water properly and then shampoo and condition. Another option is to use only olive oil and mayo, as that too helps hair shine.

4. Drink spinach juice to control hair fall.

5. For shiny hair, use vinegar+water for a final rinse.

6. Use conditioner only from your mid lengths to the ends. Not on your scalp.

7. Adding 1 tsp of baking soda in your shampoo will take out all the product build up in your hair. Do not overuse or your hair will go dry. It's best to use this formula once a month.

CARING FOR YOUR SKIN AND HAIR

Taking care of skin and hair can be done in two ways. The first way of taking care is by external methods. The second way is by consuming the right types of food. Everyone can get flawless skin and shiny hair. But what you need to focus on is long-term results. Trends come and go, and in the end they are useless. The question that is pertinent is 'How do we get long-term results and make them stay there?' My mission has always been to work from the inside out. This is an approach with results, not hope. I plan menus that will cleanse and beautify your bodies. **Your organs**

are the key. By following my menus, you will be strengthening your organs so that they function with optimum power.

If you pinch your cheeks, they'll turn red, or if you've tripped on the stairs and fallen face first in front of your colleagues, you'll blush yourself to a blood red tomato. That's because our skin is fed by our blood right from the first layer to the last, and is the thinnest on our faces. So in essence we need to improve the blood structure of our body to get glowing skin. And this can only be done by eating right.

Food plays a significant role in the beauty of your skin. Your face, skin, and hair care does not begin with a facial or a trip to the spa, but your own choices regarding what foods you will choose from now on. You will be amazed to know how healthy food habits and lifestyle can help to get a younger looking healthy skin. Food rich in saturated fat and calories is not ideal for a greater looking skin. On the contrary, food rich in iron, mineral, and vitamins is excellent for the skin. Consistent water consumption can also be beneficial, as it removes toxins from the body, making it more healthy and glowing. Regular exercising and getting enough sleep is part of a healthy lifestyle.

Here is a 7-day skin regeneration diet which benefits the skin, complete face, and the hair. Once you know the format for one day, it's a question of varying the grain, lentils, and vegetables. Just remember to do the liver flush remedy (see recipe on p 306), green smoothie, and body scrub suggested daily.

7-DAY MENU PLAN FOR SKIN AND HAIR

	Breakfast	Mid-morning	Lunch	Evening	Evening Snack	Dinner
Day 1	Millet porridge/ poha. Take 1 tsp black seed oil or tea early morning	Green smoothie with ½ tsp of spirulina and green apples. Add 2 tbs of flax seed oil	Barley (jov) rotis/ or whole green moong dal, red pumpkin (any style) Side order: sauerkraut	Melon, any berries, papaya, coconut water, almonds, walnuts	Sweet potato pancake	Soup (with miso if possible), brown rice, fenugreek (methi); you can add sweet potatoes, lentils (split) (vegetarians), fish (non vegetarians)
Day 2	Brown rice poha or brown rice porridge. Take 1 tsp black seed oil or tea early morning	Green smoothie with ½ tsp of spirulina and green apples. Add 2 tbs of flax seed oil	Millet flavoured with spices with a squeeze of lemon, chickpea curry, mustard leaves (sarson), or yellow and green peppers cooked in any style Side order: quick pickle (see p 283)	Watermelon or peaches, any berries, any melon, coconut water, nuts	Moong dal chillas	Soup (with miso if possible), amaranth (rajeera) rotis, lentils, carrots, and peas

Day					
Day 3	Millet porridge/ poha. Take 1 tsp black seed oil or tea early morning	Green smoothie with ½ tsp of spirulina and green apples. Add 2 tbs of flax seed oil	Brown rice with leafy green, red kidney bean curry, greens salad with lemon olive oil dressing. Add all kinds of greens, asparagus, and sprouts. Side order: sauerkraut	Melon, any berries, papaya, coconut water, almonds, walnuts	Hummus with veggie sticks	Soup (with miso if possible), barley (jov) rotis, or whole barley cooked in vegetable stock, mushrooms with peas, lentils, or fish
Day 4	Amaranth rotis with leafy green or brown rice porridge. Take 1 tsp black seed oil or tea early morning	Green smoothie with ½ tsp of spirulina and green apples. Add 2 tbs of flax seed oil	Brown rice cutlets, white beans in tomato base, red pumpkin sautéed with basil and garlic. Side order: quick pickle	Melon, any berries, papaya, coconut water, almonds, walnuts	Steamed green dumplings	Barley and vegetable soup, nishime-style vegetables, green moong salad

	Breakfast	Mid-morning	Lunch	Evening	Evening Snack	Dinner
Day 5	Millet poha or porridge. Take 1 tsp black seed oil or tea early morning	Green smoothie with ½ tsp of spirulina and green apples. Add 2 tbs of flax seed oil	Brown rice salad, pumpkin seed gravy with tofu (p 266) or lentils, sauteed pak choi with garlic. Side order: pressed salad	Melon, any berries, papaya, coconut water, almonds, walnuts	Sweet potato and carrot cutlets	Broccoli soup, udon noodles, tomato-base pasta sauce, soy mince balls or fish, cauliflower in lemon and tahini sauce
Day 6	Brown rice idlis or porridge. Take 1 tsp black seed oil or tea early morning	Green smoothie with ½ tsp of spirulina and green apples. Add 2 tbs of flax seed oil	Millet with vegetables, red kidney bean cutlets, arugula salad with avocado, cucumber and berries, mushroom moussaka. Side order: quick pickle	Melon, any berries, papaya, coconut water, almonds, walnuts	Use leftover brown rice, idlis, or idli atta for dosas with methi leaves	Asparagus soup (with miso if possible), amaranth rotis or brown rice, green moong with spinach, stir fry cabbage with green and yellow peppers

Day 7	Millet poha or porridge. Take 1 tsp black seed oil or tea early morning	Green smoothie with ½ tsp of spirulina and green apples. Add 2 tbs of flax seed oil	Brown rice with sesame seeds, chickpea with mustard greens (sarson), sweet potato salad. Side order: sauerkraut	Melon, any berries, papaya, coconut water, almonds, walnuts	Corn roti wrap	Cauliflower soup, barley with mushrooms, black bean salad or fish, spiced spinach

11

THE BODY DIET

'Five and a half.'

'Two.'

'Ten!'

'Four.'

And there's the occasional, 'Thirteen goddamit.'

This may seem like a brood of young women comparing 'notes' on a girl's night out but it isn't. Those figures are the numbers that women want to see decrease on the weighing machine. Here's an exercise. Try complimenting a woman. Go ahead and tell them they're looking gorgeous, and observe their reaction. It'll range from 'Oh god I look fat!' and 'Aren't my thighs looking heavy?' to 'Shut up!' It's very rarely that a woman will be gracious and thank you for it. Have you yourself ever flipped through a glossy magazine and thought: 'I could never look like that?' The thing is that no one's happy with the way they look, and a lot has to with the fact they're not feeling too happy from the inside, both in the mind and body.

Everybody wants to be in better shape. And the simple thing about it is that you can. *You absolutely can.* With the right eating habits, you can have it all. The goal of any weight-loss plan should not be about getting too thin, it should concentrate on reaching a comfortable weight that is optimal for you, your age, and body type. Remember the story of Goddess Kali biting her tongue? Like her, you must learn to control your desire for foods. My approach supplies you with rich nutrients that nourish you, curtails foods that cause a toxic overload, recommends lifestyle practices that need modification, and suggests you lead a less chaotic life. The Beauty Diet works on cleaning the blood condition, each organ, and then focuses on making the body function like the parts of a well-oiled machine. And as your body starts regaining its inner balance, weight loss will happen as a natural by product. Just remember, all your organs have to work in tandem for your body to get its balance back and you'll lose those unnecessary extra kilos without even asking for it.

Vikram Bhatt's story

Vikram was initially recommended to me by his physiotherapist. He tried my meals but could not adjust to the food and gave up in a week. He called me back three and a half years later saying he would like to give it another shot, and this time for weight loss. I knew it would be more challenging because of his various health conditions; he was struggling with fibromyalgia, migraine, and high blood pressure. His body was clearly out of balance, and that was the first thing I needed to fix. He agreed to eat all my meals, including the breakfast and evening snack, which made my job as a health counsellor easier, but more challenging as a health chef.

I gave him the basic platform of the approach: whole grains, legumes, a lot of vegetables, and good quality fermented foods. The basic approach is rich in 'seratonin boosters', and since he has fibromyalgia, I knew he needed to eat these foods daily. This time around, Vikram was enthusiastic and embraced the diet wholeheartedly, paying close attention to the what-not-to-eat list. Although I did allow him his one cup of tea with a dash of milk, I'm not quite the sergeant I make myself out to be.

Since weight loss was his objective, I upped his protein intake by adding amaranth (combined with sorghum) to give him his protein, besides the beans/lentils and whole grains. Vikram is a vegetarian, so I made sure his protein always came from good vegetables and lentils (stuffing his rotis with greens). He ate brown rice daily, but once or twice a week we included black wild rice, millet poha at breakfast, and a lot of quinoa. In the vegetable group, I made sure he had a lot of squash/red pumpkin (bhopla)—all root vegetables that are a source of fibre and complex carbohydrates and all natural serotonin boosters. His snacks were vegetable, grain, or protein based, so he had anything from a sweet potato chaat, green moong dal chillas, to green moong salad with vegetables and lots of leafy greens always thrown in. I kept it varied and interesting. To keep him happy, I occasionally gave him a granola bar made out of my kitchen, which again is rich in complex carbohydrates, nuts, and seeds. This served as an in-between snack, and if he was stuck for long hours without a meal. I added a good quality of camouflaged-fermented foods in the form of miso in soups at dinner and quick pickles and sauerkraut, to his food, because I knew he would not eat them otherwise. However, I did not take him off whole grain at night because when you work hard, you must replenish your body's strength through the foods you eat. It's the fuel to keep you going. Especially vital because Vikram had no time to exercise. I also supplemented his diet with spirulina and wheat grass, and used flax seed oil and chia seeds in the meals. More importantly, he was in the pre-release phase of his movie *Haunted*, so I could not influence his lifestyle that much. He kept awake at nights, and did not get much sleep, which is a killer for weight loss.

Vikram lost five kilos in the first month itself.

WHAT VIKRAM HAS TO SAY ABOUT THE BEAUTY DIET:

'My first tryst with Shonali's approach to food did not go as well as planned. I found the food different, and it was difficult to shift from my normal diet to the more structured and natural way to food and health. My second attempt was hugely successful, and I realized that this was the only way that one can make a difference to one's health. Kind of like the whole horse and taking it to drink the water deal.

I suffer from several ailments like fibromyalgia, migraine, and high blood pressure, but Shonali was able to use the food like a medicine and help me with those conditions. I slept better and felt better. To add to it, I understood that taste is a matter of habit. People all over the world have different taste preferences according to the region where they are born in, which means that taste is not inborn but cultivated. So also in this case, once you acquire it, the taste becomes a part of your everyday life.

Modern science has a medicine for everything, well almost everything. But if you look closely, you'll realize that medicines are more for symptomatic relief than curing you completely. They'll cure your headache but not the cause, they'll give you sleep with a pill, and kill your other aches and pains with more pills. This approach helps in the actual cure, not just in the relief. And that is of utmost importance.

VIKRAM BHATT—BOLLYWOOD DIRECTOR, PRODUCER,
AND SCREENWRITER

Weight control is a life issue that requires sustaining rather than temporary improvement, followed by disappointment. In order to keep your weight stable, you should follow the basic foods suggested in this approach; just remember the closer you are to a plant-based approach, the more you will keep your weight off and stay healthy.

Losing weight as a natural by product comes by understanding two things:

1) The balanced approach to food that is, mainly a plant-based (vegetarian) approach with a lower proportion of meats in your diet.
2) Understanding your organs and what foods benefit them individually.

A RECAP OF THE APPROACH (SEE PICTURE)

> Whole grains: 30 percent
> Legumes/Fish: 30 percent
> Vegetables: 25 to 30 percent (of which 5 percent are fermented foods and 5 percent soups)
> Fruit: 5 to 10 percent
> Nuts and seeds: 2.5 percent
> Other: 2.5 percent (herbal teas, quick pickles, condiments).

Remember, you should avoid coffees, teas (Indian tea), sugar, processed foods, white flour alcohol, meats, dairy, and bad quality fats. This should see you do your home run on a daily basis and on keeping your system working tickety boo. Refer to the picture below to see you balanced approach.

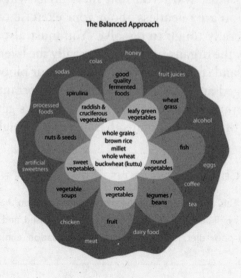

The Balanced Approach

The other tenet of this approach is to eat according to how your organs will be nourished; this not only impacts that particular organ, but cleans up your energy pathways, namely the meridians or the nadis (in the Indian system). Foods that cause mucous in the body block these pathways and you develop problems from bad skin, hair fall, weight gain, and other major health issues. Each organ works with other organs, so it's not one organ that you will need to focus on. For example, if you have skin issues, you know that the liver affects the skin; so you must know specific food groups that additionally help rejuvenate the liver. Your diet must rest on a foundation that impacts all organs.

The general approach I recommend helps all the organs to function well; therefore all the problem areas such as the hips/thighs in women and belly/love handles in men, or any other area where you are accumulating fat, will be affected. I must warn you that these areas will respond better if you are relentless about your exercise regime as fat is generally tough to dissolve. You must also keep in mind how the organs function, especially the liver, spleen/pancreas, and stomach, as that is where your blood sugars are managed and nutrients absorbed—important factors in you getting to your optimal weight. So let's get a basic overview of the main organs that help with weight loss.

CELLULITE, LET ME COUNT THE WAYS WE HATE THEE

This unsightly bumpy appearance of cellulite on the skin is dreaded by all alike. Cellulite is not a fat but skin issue, and occurs due to a poor diet. It results from poor circulation, elimination, lymphatic drainage, and insufficient exercise. A precondition for cellulite is the build up of wastes in the body by bad eating habits, which get trapped in the cells and in and around tissues.

So how do you get rid of it?

- Start with the detox diet.
- Keep the key mantra of grains, greens, beans, fish and good quality fermented foods in mind, as it focuses on generating good blood quality, elimination of toxins, and assimilation of nutrients.
- Avoid sugars, processed foods, dairy, meats, eggs, poultry, refined flours, and processed foods like the plague.
- Exercise, exercise, exercise—especially aerobic activity—at least three times a week.
- Add pranayam to your daily routine. It helps to detoxify and oxygenate your blood.
- When you do the body scrub, make sure you rub the cellulite-ridden areas well, to aid the discharge of old foods and toxins.

The vital organs

THE LIVER

At one time the liver was considered the seat of life; hence its name—liver, the thing we live with. It is one of the most important organs, as it is a large filtering unit. Everything we ingest passes through the liver. And it will hang on to the residue of all the medication which we have taken throughout our life. The fats from dairy, animal foods, flour products, fried foods, refined oils, all weaken the liver.

Signs that your liver isn't working properly:

- Lack of sleep

- Over exhaustion
- If you feel sleepy after eating
- In case you are up between 1 to 2 am in the morning and harbour negative thoughts at this time or are worried
- If you have the urge to urinate late at night, usually between 1 am to 3 am
- Inflamed eyes
- Your tendons are sore or tear easily
- Constant anger, impatience, and irritation

Keeping the liver healthy goes hand-in-hand with keeping your stomach healthy and clean and is an important precursor to keeping your weight stable, have great skin and hair. (See the liver foods in the chart attached for organs and their foods on p 121). Blanching, pressed (salads), quick sautés, quick pickles, and boiling as opposed to pressure cooking are cooking styles that will benefit your liver.

THE LUNGS AND LARGE INTESTINE

The relationship between the lungs and large intestine is an important one. One of the ways to keep your excretory system functioning well is to also have a healthy lung function. If your lungs are deficient in any way, chances are you will always have a problem in your stomach. You will be constipated as the large intestine will be affected. The reverse of this is also true; so if your large intestine does not function well, and food stagnates here, lung function is also affected. Bad skin would be a result of both these organs being in a state of imbalance. So it's absolutely imperative to keep your stomach clean and have healthy lungs. Your lungs process gases, which are eliminated from your large intestine; so if you are not eating food which is being assimilated, an unusual amount of carbon dioxide builds up which the lungs find difficult to process.

The lungs and large intestine are connected, as body fluids are governed by the lungs. Healthy lungs mean radiant-looking skin and hair and vice versa. A strong voice is also indicative of healthy lungs.

Foods that put pressure on the lungs: All yeast products (bread, cakes, alcohol), dairy, honey, antibiotics, any food colours, foods high in fats and sugars.

Beneficial cooking styles: Slow cooking styles like grilling, nishime, baking, and longer sautés/boiling are beneficial to the lungs and large intestine.

See remedies for the lungs in the Recipe section.

WEIGHT-LOSS REMEDY FOR NON VEGETARIANS

Try this remedy every other day for three weeks to start the process and then two to three times a week for two weeks, then stop. Do not do it if you are weak or have just come out of an illness or are recovering from one. You can do it anytime of the day that suits you.

See Recipe section for the Carrot and White Radish remedy.

A week in the life of losing your weight

Once you get the hang of the basic approach to the Beauty Diet, you will know what you need to work with. Keep in mind the Beauty Diet key (grains, greens, beans, good fermented foods) and what not to avoid. If you keep the pointers in mind, you will know how to work it out for your entire week, as per your palette and taste.

	Breakfast	Mid-morning	Lunch	Mid-afternoon	Evening snack	Dinner
Day 1	Millet porridge/ poha	Fruit any (except bananas) (gap of 1½ hour post breakfast) and green smoothie with ½ tsp of spirulina (½ glass only); add 2 tbsp flax oil	Barley (joy) rotis/or brown rice, green moong dal, red pumpkin with garlic and basil. Side order: quick pickle and a carrot radish condiment	Sweet vegetable drink, carrot mooli drink (for non vegetarians), and a little later a sweet vegetable drink	Hummus with veggie sticks or fruit	Cauliflower soup (with miso if possible), lentil soup or steamed fish, fenugreek (methi) with sweet potatoes. Before bed: 1 tbsp black seed oil in hot water or tea* (see recipe)
Day 2	Brown rice poha or porridge	Fruit any (except bananas) (gap of 1½ hour post breakfast) and green smoothie with ½ tsp of spirulina (½ glass only); add 2 tbsp flax oil	Millet and veggies with a squeeze of lemon, chickpea with leafy greens. Mustard leaves (sarson) or spinach. Side order: pressed salad	Sweet vegetable drink, carrot mooli drink (for non vegetarians), and a little later, a sweet vegetable drink	Leafy green dumplings or fruit	Tomato shorba (with miso if possible), black or white bean salad, green peppers with tofu. Before bed: 1 tbsp black seed oil in hot water or tea* (see

Day						
Day 3	Millet porridge/poha or amaranth rotis with leafy green vegetable	Fruit any (except bananas) (gap of 1½ hour post breakfast) and green smoothie with ½ tsp of spirulina (½ glass only); add 2 tbsp flax oil	Brown rice with leafy greens, red kidney bean curry, green salad with lemon-olive oil dressing; add: all kinds of greens, asparagus, and sprouts. Side order: sauerkraut and carrot radish condiment	Sweet vegetable drink, carrot mooli drink (for non vegetarians), and a little later, a sweet vegetable drink	Sweet potato pancakes or fruit	Squash soup (with miso if possible), mushroom moussaka with tofu or steamed/grilled fish, carrots with peas. Before bed: 1 tbsp black seed oil in hot water or tea* (see recipe)
Day 4	Brown rice porridge	Fruit any (except bananas) (gap of 1½ hour post breakfast), green smoothie with ½ tsp of spirulina (½ glass only); add 2 tbsp flax oil	Millet with veggies, white beans in tomato base, arugula and veggie salad. Side order: quick pickle	Sweet vegetable drink, carrot mooli drink (for non vegetarians), and a little later, a sweet vegetable drink	Moong dal chillas (pancakes) or fruit	Barley and vegetable soup (miso) Nishime-style vegetables, green moong salad. Before bed: 1 tbsp black seed oil in hot water or tea* (see recipe)

	Breakfast	Mid-morning	Lunch	Mid-afternoon	Evening snack	Dinner
Day 5	Millet poha or porridge	Fruit any (except bananas) (gap of 1½ hour post breakfast) and green smoothie with ½ tsp of spirulina (½ glass only); add 2 tbsp flax oil	Brown rice salad, white bean salad, sauteed pak choi with garlic, or fenugreek with carrots. Side order: pressed salad and carrot radish condiment	Sweet vegetable drink, carrot mooli drink (for non vegetarians), and alittle later a sweet vegetable drink	Bean cutlets with chutney	Broccoli soup (with miso if possible), White soybean (protein) salad, cauliflower with cumin scented oil, or steamed fish, Before bed: 1 tbsp black seed oil in hot water or tea* (see recipe)
Day 6	Brown rice idlis or porridge	Fruit any (except bananas) (gap of 1½ hour post breakfast) and green smoothie with ½ tsp of spirulina (½ glass	Millet with vegetables, red kidney bean cutlets, pumpkin seed gravy, arugula salad with avocado, cucumber and berries.	Sweet vegetable drink, carrot mooli drink (for non vegetarians), a and little later a sweet vegetable drink	Corn on the cob or fruit	Bohemian soup (with miso if possible), green moong with spinach, cabbage in coriander sauce. Before bed: 1 tbsp

		only); add 2 tbsp flax oil	Side order: quick pickle			black seed oil in hot water or tea* (see recipe)
Day 7	Millet poha or porridge	Fruit any (except bananas) (gap of 1½ hour post breakfast) and green smoothie with ½ tsp of spirulina (½ glass only); add 2 tbsp flax oil	Brown rice with greens, dal with mushrooms and green peppers, garlic French beans. Side order: sauerkraut, carrot radish condiment	Sweet vegetable drink, carrot mooli drink (for non vegetarians), and a little later, a sweet vegetable drink	Falafel with chutney	Doodhi (gourd) soup (with miso if possible), scrambled tofu or steamed fish, spiced fenugreek (methi). Before bed: 1 tbsp black seed oil in hot water or tea* (see recipe)

* It is optional to consume black seed oil at night.

Contradictions for the use of flax oil/seed: Flax seed or oil may slow your body's absorption rate for medications that you may be on, so avoid taking it at the same time as these medications; if you are on blood thinners, and blood sugar lowering medication, do not take flax seed or flax oil.

Snack suggestions for healthy weight

Try these snack ideas that are delicious and healthy and won't create havoc on your weight goals (apart from the ones mentioned in the snack section of the book):

1. Fresh vegetables with a dip like hummus, baba ghanoush, or tofu mayonnaise. Add fresh herbs and seasonings for more flavour
2. Roasted nuts and seeds
3. Fruit plain or with good-quality yoghurt (if you eat dairy, see fruit combination list for fruits which you can combine with dairy) and freshly ground flax seed or chia seeds
4. Whole-grain crackers with a small piece of aged cheese or smoked salmon
5. If you eat eggs: a hardboiled egg sprinkled with seasonings
6. Millet poha
7. Steamed muthiya made with cabbage and leafy greens
8. Steamed or boiled vegetables with salad dressing (homemade)

9. Green moong dal chillas with chutney
10. Falafel or bean cutlets
11. Corn bhel
12. Chickpea, green moong, or sweet potato with chaat masala

12

THE ANTI-AGEING DIET

Before we proceed to fighting ageing, let's get a sense of how young or old your body is. It's like a reality check. Don't skip it. It's always good to know the truth about your body. And be honest.

The How-Young-are-You? quiz

1) Can you walk up two flights of stairs without pausing?

    a. Yes

    b. Sometimes

    c. Why take the stairs when there's something called the elevator?

2) How well do you handle stress?

    a. My friends say I'm a rock

    b. I feel frazzled on busy days, but otherwise I'm okay.

    c. I'm 'Panic Jane' on most days

3) How many servings of nuts (a serving is about an ounce or a small fistful) have you eaten in the last three days?

    a. 0

    b. 2

    c. 3 or more

4) How many days a week do you take a thirty-minute walk?

    a. 7

    b. 3 or 4

    c. Do trips from the couch to the refrigerator count?

5) You eat out...

    a. only if there's an occasion that I just must attend. But never otherwise.

    b. once a week at least

    c. Are you kidding me? Take out always.

6) When was the last time you changed your skin-care routine?

    a. About six months ago

    b. So long ago, I can't remember

    c. Routine? Who has time for that?

7) Fish, chicken, or red meat?

    a. Fish

    b. Chicken

    c. The red stuff

8) How many cigarettes?

    a. Don't touch the stuff

    b. Once in a while

    c. I carry a packet with me wherever I go

9) How likely are you to fall asleep in the middle of doing something else like reading, watching TV, sitting in a movie theatre, or in a meeting? How likely are you to fall asleep while talking to someone, sitting quietly after lunch, or when caught in traffic?

    a. Unlikely

    b. Somewhat likely

    c. Very likely

10) How many days a week do you get a good night's sleep of at least 6½ hours?

    a. 7

    b. 3–6

    c. 0–2 but after two glasses of wine.

Mostly As: Congratulations! You're an infant and probably have the metabolism of a 14 year old. You've been good to your body, and guess what, your body will be good to you in return, keeping you younger for longer. What you need to do is to keep it up. The process of ageing is only natural and we all have to go through it. However, you seem to know what to do.

Mostly Bs: You're walking the fine line between being healthy and slipping. You know what you have to do but probably get caught with the rush of everyday life, juggling work and personal life. Take some time out and reevaluate your priorities. Planning is key. With a little bit of organizing, you can get back on track and get your health in order. It isn't too much to ask for if you want to keep fit and stay younger.

Mostly Cs: Whoa! You have to put the brakes on your life and slow it down several notches. Right now your life is mad with activity and you're paying no attention to your body, the thing that's sustaining you. You've got to take a hold of the situation before it slips out of control. Remember, your body is your temple and it is what's going to get you through till the end. The first thing you need to do is fix your eating habits. Trust me, once you do that, everything else starts to fall in place. Next would be exercise. No need to hit the gym or take up martial arts classes. Start with baby steps. Take the stairs instead of the elevator. Go fetch your own print outs. Walk to the supermarket instead of driving. Just start using those limbs. You need to take stock if you don't want the first wrinkle arriving before you hit thirty five.

'Nature gives you the face you have when you are twenty. Life gives you the face you have when you are thirty; it's up to you to merit the face you have at fifty.'

—Coco Chanel

While it's a known fact that genetics play a huge role in keeping us looking younger, a larger component in ageing is how we choose to eat and live. At a very young age I became conscious of making the right food choices. I remember being active in sports in school and also pretty high on Jane Fonda, kickboxing, step aerobics, and swimming after I was fifteen. I must admit here that even though I came from a home where the meat, eggs, and dairy consumption was high, somehow my good karma made me veer off these things in my late twenties and I started incorporating healthy foods, which I learnt of through books and my passion for health. I met Dr Vijaya Venkat and began practicing her approach, which was immensely helpful. I didn't realize that slowly, but surely, I was laying the foundation of stalling my ageing process. I don't suffer from pimples, hair fall, and have never had to seek beauty treatments. I have learnt that my body is at a happy weight; so as long as I feel fit and strong from inside, it's all that matters. I have immense amounts of energy, and don't feel that's changed much since my teens. Over the years I have become more routine oriented and I guess that comes with the discipline of work and the fact that one is committed to one's own health.

Of course, my training in macrobiotics took it to another level: I have not consumed sugar, dairy, yeast, processed food, meat, or table salt since 2004. I have never really felt old, as age to me is just a number and that has not affected me. However, when people around me get to know my age and react to the fact that I look ten years younger than I actually am, they get up and pay attention to what the foods have done for me. Of course, my methods are stringent for some, but then I have learnt how to balance myself out and have been successful at doing so.

Today, looking beautiful is a whole different ball game. It's not just about being gorgeous, it's about looking *younger* which has taken precedence. What we must understand is that ageing is the natural process of life. All of us will age. There's just no stopping it, unless you're heading down the botox path, which I will never recommend. But what we can do is retard the process of ageing. Being healthy can be achieved by eating right and exercising; but to control ageing, we need to be overtly aware of our bodies and give it triple the regular care. Let's start with where it all begins—the kidneys, the powerhouse for energy.

The kidneys, vitality, and ageing

The kidneys are responsible for the 'healthy glow of health'. They are responsible for your youth, vitality (even sexual), mental vigour, and help maintain hair, bones, and teeth. At the time of your conception, the kidneys store the essence derived from your parents. This essence determines your basic constitution, hence they are described as the 'root of life', and control the decay of the body. However, the essence you inherit from your parents is only partially responsible for the health of your body. While you inherit 20 percent of it from your parents, 80 percent is actually maintained by the foods you eat. (Refer to the chart on next page for specific kidney foods).

This essence is also referred to as the jing in Traditional Chinese Medicine. While the Beauty Diet nourishes this jing automatically, you can also add other foods to your diet to build up this vitality. Any foods which are high in nucleic acids, which protect the body's degeneration, will nourish this jing. Nucleic acids promotes the body's own rejuvenation process, helping it to repair itself, remove toxins, and produce more energy.

All hormones are made from a raw material which initially comes from your kidneys and adrenals. If your kidneys are under stress due to poor quality foods, overwork, excessive sexual activity, excessive alcohol, tobacco, or drugs, they will fail to produce these hormones, so essential for the underlying functions in your body. This approach focusses on making natural versions of melatonin, natural DHEA, and trytophan.

Your Attractiveness Dimensions Impacted by Specific Foods

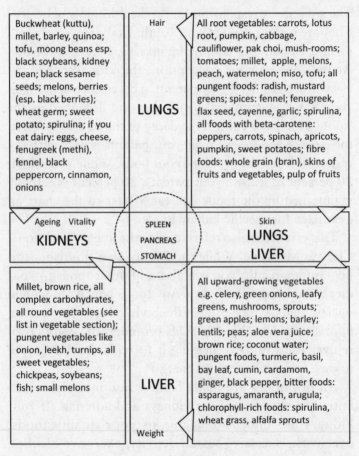

Buckwheat (kuttu), millet, barley, quinoa; tofu, moong beans esp. black soybeans, kidney bean; black sesame seeds; melons, berries (esp. black berries); wheat germ; sweet potato; spirulina; if you eat dairy: eggs, cheese, fenugreek (methi), fennel, black peppercorn, cinnamon, onions

Hair

LUNGS

All root vegetables: carrots, lotus root, pumpkin, cabbage, cauliflower, pak choi, mush-rooms; tomatoes; millet, apple, melons, peach, watermelon; miso, tofu; all pungent foods: radish, mustard greens; spices: fennel; fenugreek, flax seed, cayenne, garlic; spirulina, all foods with beta-carotene: peppers, carrots, spinach, apricots, pumpkin, sweet potatoes; fibre foods: whole grain (bran), skins of fruits and vegetables, pulp of fruits

Ageing Vitality
KIDNEYS

SPLEEN
PANCREAS
STOMACH

Skin
LUNGS
LIVER

Millet, brown rice, all complex carbohydrates, all round vegetables (see list in vegetable section); pungent vegetables like onion, leekh, turnips, all sweet vegetables; chickpeas, soybeans; fish; small melons

LIVER

Weight

All upward-growing vegetables e.g. celery, green onions, leafy greens, mushrooms, sprouts; green apples; lemons; barley; lentils; peas; aloe vera juice; brown rice; coconut water; pungent foods, turmeric, basil, bay leaf, cumin, cardamom, ginger, black pepper, bitter foods: asparagus, amaranth, arugula; chlorophyll-rich foods: spirulina, wheat grass, alfalfa sprouts

NATURAL **DHEA** (DEHYDROEPIANDROSTERONE)

DHEA is a hormone that is naturally made by the human body. Also called the 'youth hormone', it is a precursor to every other hormone your body will need. DHEA is used for slowing or reversing ageing, improving thinking skills in older people, and slowing the progress of Alzheimer's disease. It helps form the hormones estrogen and testosterone. It is also responsible for body functions such as fat and mineral metabolism, and stress control. Since the Beauty Diet lays emphasis on the proper functioning of your kidneys and adrenals, be assured that you will get an abundance of DHEA from it.

Foods that put pressure on the kidneys: Ice and ice-cold drinks, raw foods (in excess), excessive salt (table salt), dairy foods, and sugars.

Cooking styles that nourish the kidneys: Stewing, pressure cooking, baking, deep frying, all warming styles like boiling rice, then stir frying it with vegetables, longer pickling, and stews.

A good spiritual practice like meditation, or any other practices that keeps you in touch with your inner self, are essential to keep the kidney's 'essence' going.

TIPS ON KEEPING THE KIDNEYS HEALTHY

Focus on all liver-regenerating foods such as micro algae (spirulina), all fish, (although sardines contain one of the highest levels of nucleic acids, accounting for 1.5 percent of its nutritional components), cereal grass like wheat grass, liver (if you eat meat), ghee (supports ojas as described in the Ayurvedic tradition which is their way of addressing this jing), almond milk or almonds, tofu/soybean, spinach, leek, broccoli, chinese cabbage, and cauliflower. These contain high levels of nucleic acids, while mushrooms, especially shiitake, chia, and flaxseeds, contain Omega 3.

FACTORS THAT WILL EXHAUST YOUR ESSENCE

1. Too much sexual activity
2. Overwork and stress
3. Fear and insecurity (these are the emotions of the kidneys)
4. Toxic overload from foods, environment, alcohol, drugs, tobacco, and excessive protein intake (for example whey protein will exhaust kidneys over time)
5. Too much sugar
6. Irregularity in lifestyle and eating

See Recipe section for remedies for the kidney

Ginger compress (External remedy for the kidney)

This is an extremely powerful external remedy, and I have used it periodically myself. If you are manifesting fear and insecurity, or feel that your kidneys are overworked (signs of which are being tired all the time, lack energy, and dark circles around your eyes), you can use this external treatment. It is also extremely good for aches and pains that you may have in your body.

A word of caution: Don't use this remedy if you have a very serious condition such as cancer, or are pregnant. Do not use it around the head area, or when you are running a temperature.

Method:

Grate about a golf ball-sized piece of ginger, place it on a muslin cloth, and tie a knot. Boil a pot full of water, squeeze the juice of the ginger into the water, and then place the muslin in it. Keep it soaked while you do the compress. Keep two hand towels ready, dip one into the water, in the centre, but keep the ends dry so you can wring the water (as it will be very hot), and place the wet part on the kidney area (the lower back). Cover with a dry towel to keep the heat trapped inside. Replace the wet towel, with another wet towel, every three to four minutes. Repeat this process for up to five times, this will take twenty minutes.

Note: A ginger compress can be used for the following problems—asthma (on the chest), bronchitis, digestive disorders, jaundice, muscle pain, and stomach cramps.

Signs to watch out for if your organs are healing

Liver	Lesser acidity, gas, clearer skin, better sleep, lesser anger, being more creative
Lungs/large intestine	Lesser colds, coughs, sinus issues, regular bowels, clearer skin, happier disposition
Kidneys	Lesser hair fall, no water retention, clear urine, more energy, less fear

Spleen/pancreas/ stomach	No sugar cravings, lesser acidity, lesser mood swings, strong immunity, no anxiety
Heart/small intestine	Healthy complexion, lower blood pressure, more joyous and relaxed

Spleen, pancreas, and the stomach

The spleen, pancreas, and stomach are the central organs in the production and extraction of nutrients required by the body, forming the basis of a good or bad blood condition. They are often referred to as the 'granary officials'—the centre of everything. They regulate blood flow and maintain blood-sugar levels, regulate water metabolism and help to circulate water in the body.

A balance in these organs will help all your organs function better resulting in an ideal weight, great skin, lustrous hair, vitality, and youthfulness. If they are not in harmony, you may either be overweight or too thin, you may have a pale complexion, brittle nails, or suffer lethargy or mood swings. (Refer to chart for foods that benefit these organs on p 121).

Foods that put pressure on the spleen, pancreas, and stomach: Sugars, honey, excessive fruit and fruit juices, food colour/additives, processed foods, and refined flours.

Cooking styles that nourish the spleen, pancreas, and stomach: Faster cooked stews, medium boils, nishime, longer steaming of foods, and pressed foods like salads.

So while foods that aid in keeping these organs in good health are the basis on which this approach is built, you can also add the foods listed below to your daily diet. The foods are mainly complex carbohydrates that give you both insoluble and soluble fiber, required to keep your insides clean. Your focus in maintaining a sound dietary approach and lifestyle practices must include having regular bowel movements.

Black seed oil or black seed tea kalonji helps with immunity, the digestive system, liver, and issues related to skin and hair. To make black seed tea, add 1 tbs to boiling hot water. Cover and allow it to steep for ten minutes. Drink warm.

Beauty secret: Beta Carotene (see p 200) protects you from free radical damage which will cause your skin to age faster and also build collagen. Find it in natural food sources like spinach, sweet potatoes, tomatoes, yellow bell peppers, squash (bhopla), carrots, mangoes, apricots, melons, and all plants rich in chlorophyll. Chlorophyll activates enzymes which produce Vitamin E and K, and helps convert carotene to Vitamin A required for smooth skin and great hair, teeth, and bones.

Foods that will dim your vitality and cause you to age faster: Sugar, jaggery, honey, sweeteners; dairy and dairy products (includes paneer, chass, cheese, and yoghurt); refined flour (includes bread, pasta made with refined flour); meat; eggs; coffee and black Indian tea; alcohol, processed and packaged foods; chocolates; stimulants; sweets; baked products; refined oils; and fruit juices.

A week in the life of age control

Anti-AGEING DIET

	Early Morning	Breakfast	Mid-morning	Lunch	Mid-afternoon	Evening snack	Dinner
Day 1	Chia seeds (½ tsp soaked overnight), 1 shot of wheat grass juice	Millet, poha, or porridge	Fruit (except bananas) (gap of 1½ hour post breakfast) and 2 tbs of flax oil in half a glass of water. Note: read contraindications on flax	Barley (jov) rotis/or brown rice, green moong salad, pumpkin seed curry with carrots, Side order: quick pickle Note: add 1 tsp gomashio over brown rice	Sweet vegetable drink, ½ tsp of spirulina in a glass of water, 5 almonds and 5 walnuts	Sweet potato pancakes or khakra with chutney	Spinach beetroot soup (with miso if possible), split lentils with spices or fish (any style), fenugreek (methi) with carrots, brown rice or rotis and quick pickle. Before bed: 1 tbsp black seed oil in hot water or tea* (see recipe)

| Day 2 | Chia seeds (½ tsp soaked overnight) 1 shot of wheat grass juice | Brown rice, poha, or porridge | Fruit(except bananas) (gap of 1½ hour post breakfast) and 2 tbs of flax oil in half a glass of warm water | Millet with veggies, chickpea with greens, mustard leaves (sarson), or spinach Side order: pressed salad note: add gomashio 1 tsp over millet | Sweet vegetable drink, ½ tsp of spirulina in a glass of water, 5 almonds and 5 walnuts | Leafy green dumplings or Fruit or roti roll with veggie | Tomato shorba with miso (if possible), split lentils, green peppers with tofu, brown rice or rotis and quick pickle. *Before bed: 1 tbsp black seed oil in hot water or tea* |
| Day 3 | Chia seeds (½ tsp soaked overnight) 1 shot of wheat grass juice | Millet, porridge/ poha | Fruit (except bananas) (gap of 1½ hour post breakfast) and 2 tbs of flax oil in half glass of warm water | Brown rice with leafy green, red kidney bean curry, red pumpkin (bhopla) made in any style | Sweet vegetable drink, ½ tsp of spirulina in a glass of water, 5 almonds and 5 walnuts | Moong dal chillas (pancakes) or fruit | Squash (bhopla) soup (with miso if possible), mushroom moussaka with tofu or steamed/grilled fish, carrots |

	Early Morning	Breakfast	Mid-morning	Lunch	Mid-afternoon	Evening snack	Dinner
				Side order: sauerkraut Note: add 1 tsp gomashio over millet			with peas, amaranth (rajeera) and jovar rotis with quick pickle. Before bed: 1 tbsp black seed oil in hot water or tea*
Day 4	Chia seeds (½ tsp soaked overnight), 1 shot of wheat grass juice	Brown rice porridge or brown rice poha	Fruit (except bananas) (gap of 1½ hour post breakfast) and 2 tbs of flax oil in a half glass of warm water	Millet with veggies, white beans in tomato base, cabbage in green sauce. Side order: quick pickle note: add gomashio 1 tsp over millet	Sweet vegetable drink, ½ tsp of spirulina in a glass of water, 5 almonds and 5 walnuts		Cauliflower soup (with miso if possible), spinach with spices, split lentils, rotis or brown rice, and quick pickle. Before bed: 1 tbsp black seed oil in hot water or tea*

Day 5	Chia seeds (½ tsp soaked overnight) 1 shot of wheat grass juice	Millet poha or Porridge	Fruit (except bananas) (gap of 1½ hour post breakfast) and 2 tbs of flax oil in half a glass of warm water	Brown rice, green moong dal with spinach, paapri aloo chaat. Side order: Pressed salad Note: add gomashio 1 tsp over brown rice	Sweet vegetable drink, ½ tsp of spirulina in a glass of water, 5 almonds and 5 walnuts	Bean cutlets with chutney	Broccoli soup (with miso if possible), split lentils, cauliflower cooked in any style, or steamed fish Before bed: 1 tbsp black seed oil in hot water or tea*
Day 6	Chia seeds (½ tsp soaked overnight) 1 shot of wheat grass juice	Brown rice idlis or porridge	Fruit (except bananas) (gap of 1½ hour post breakfast) and 2 tbs of flax oil in half a glass of warm water	Millet with vegetables, brown lentils (masoor), beetroot salad Side order: quick pickle	Sweet vegetable drink, ½ tsp of spirulina in a glass of water, 5 almonds and 5 walnuts	Corn on the cob or fruit or khakra with chutney	Mulligatawny soup (with miso if possible), split lentils with green peppers/ mushrooms, any leafy green veggie, rotis or brown rice,

	Early Morning	Breakfast	Mid-morning	Lunch	Mid-afternoon	Evening snack	Dinner
				Note: add gomashio 1 tsp over millet			and quick pickle Before bed: 1 tbsp black seed oil in hot water or tea*
Day 7	Chia seeds (½ tsp soaked) overnight) 1 shot of wheat grass juice	Millet, poha, or porridge	Fruit any (except bananas) (gap of 1½ hour post breakfast) and 2 tbs of flax oil in a half glass of warm water Note: read contraindications on flax	Brown rice with greens, any lentils; add red pumpki to it, green beans (any style) Side order: sauerkraut	Sweet vegetable drink, ½ tsp of spirulina in a glass of water, 5 almonds and 5 walnuts	Falafel with chutney	Doodhi (gourd) soup (with miso if possible), tofu vindaloo (steamed), spiced fenugreek (methi), brown rice, and quick pickle Before bed: 1 tbsp black seed oil in hot water or tea*

* It is optional to consume black seed oil at night.

Brown Rice Salad (see p 259)

Nishime (see p 263)

Red Pumpkin Garlic Basil (see p 265)

Red Bean Cutlets (see p 276)

Pressed Salad (see p 279)

Green Smoothie (see p 293)

Broccoli Soup (see p 297)

Baked Pear (see p 310)

Neha Dhupia loves the healthy probiotic drinks

Neha Dhupia enjoying her meals

Kabir Bedi making his morning cup of healthy green tea

Jacqueline having Shonali's lunch in between her shoot

Dalip Tahil doing organic vegetable shopping

Dalip at the veggie mart

Shonali with her food

Shonali on her graduation day at The Kushi Institute, USA, with Michio Kushi (second from left), founder of the macrobiotics diet

Shonali cooking in her kitchen

PART THREE

13

Chef Speak: Kitchen FAQs

In my experience as a chef, I've come across many people asking me very similar questions. Their answers are usually quite simple, but tend to confuse people, as everyone has a different opinion. I've put together some of those questions. They might help you the next time you're in the kitchen.

Q: How long can I eat leftovers?

You can carry leftovers for up to two meals. So today's lunch can be carried over till tomorrow's breakfast. I usually make one soup a day and use it for two meals. Leftover greens can be tossed with lime or good quality vinegar and eaten two meals after.

Q: My maid cuts the fruit I have for breakfast, the evening before and keeps it in a bowl with a clingfilm. Is it still nutritious the next morning?

Fruits are usually best when cut fresh. Polyphenol oxidase (also called tyrosinase) is an enzyme found in a fruit's cells. When the cut fruit is exposed to the air, this enzyme reacts with the oxygen. This reaction is called oxidation and causes fresh cut fruit to turn brown. So if you do cut fruits much before you eat them, squeeze some lime on it and cover it with a foil or clingfilm. Lime or anthing citrus will prevent oxidation.

Q: Should we be switching cooking oils regularly?

Not necessarily. As long as you are using a healthy cooking oil, it's fine.

Q: My maid shops for vegetables only twice a week. Is it okay to store veggies for a couple of days?

Ideally, you should shop every day. But twice a week vegetable and fruit shopping is fine. Just as long as you are sure of the quality of what you are buying. Leafy greens will not keep for a week, so you will need to shop for these more frequently.

Q: What is the best way to store veggies? How do I get the maximum benefit out of them?

Greens need to be untied, aired, and stored loosely in bags that have holes in them for ventilation. Crisper veggies like carrots and other roots can be stored in the vegetable drawer of the fridge; wrapping them up will hasten spoiling. Fruits should stay in the fridge, especially those of the more delicate variety such as grapes, peaches, and berries.

Q: How do we prevent spices and pulses from getting spoilt (getting infected with worms or acquiring an odour) in the summer?

Take a bay leaf (tej patta) and stick it on the underside of your spice container lid to keep bugs and moisture away. Even neem leaves do the trick.

Q: For how long can we keep dried chillies, bay leaf, dry mint, etc.? Do they have an expiry date?

About two months and then restock. If you buy them from your local grocer, they will not have an expiry date. A branded product will list the expiry date on the package.

Q: How long can uncooked fish marinated in salt and turmeric be stored in the freezer?

For a maximum of one hour, otherwise the marinate breaks into the fish and will make it mushy when cooked.

Q: Do we cut veggies and wash or wash them and cut?

Wash, cut, and use. Fruits and veggies have a natural coating that keeps moisture inside; so if you cut them and keep them too long, they lose this moisture and dry out. Remember to use as soon as you can after cutting.

Q. How do I store tofu?

You store tofu in an airtight container and pour filtered water on the tofu block till it is submerged in water completely. Change water once in two days.

Q. How do I get spinach to keep its colour?

Blanch it in hot water before you use it in your cooking.

Q. How do I get green peas to retain their colour?

Add a sweetener like stevia (pinch) to it while it boils.

Q. What is the best way to store leafy greens?

In my experience, a newspaper is the best way to store the freshness of leafy greens. Celery stores better if wrapped in aluminium foil.

Q. How do you make wooden chopping boards last, instead of water getting into them and they splitting?

Don't wash the every time you use them. Instead wipe down with a dry cloth, and oil them regularly—which means dip cotton in oil and rub all over the chopping board.

Q. How do I prevent dough from sticking to my rolling pin when making a base for a pizza or pie?

Stick the dough in the freezer wrapped in cling film or even the fridge for a while (about fifteen minutes) before using it.

Q. How do I ripen fruits or avocados?

Wrap them in a newspaper for few days, they will ripen faster.

Q. How do I separate noodles after they are cooked?

Add some cold water once you have drained out the hot water, this will stop the cooking process and also help to keep them separate.

14

RECIPES

ALTERNATIVES TO REGULAR MILK

1) Brown Rice Milk

Get all the benefits of brown rice from this milk.

SERVES 4

Ingredients

½ cup cooked brown rice

4 cups water

½ tsp vanilla extract

Method

1. Cook all ingredients together; could be pressure cooked as well.

2. Once cooked, blend in a mixer until smooth.

3. Then sieve through a cheesecloth/muslin cloth.

4. The residue can be used in your atta for rotis.
5. The portion that is sieved through the cloth is your rice milk.

2) All-Natural Almond Milk

This delicious, creamy milk is free from harmful vegetable oil, concentrated sweeteners, and the problems associated with both cow's milk and soy milk.

SERVES 4

Ingredients

1 ½ cups of raw almonds, soaked in water overnight
4 cups of filtered or spring water
3 to 5 dates (optional)

Method

1. Blend the almonds in 4 cups of water; you can put in the dates if you like your milk with a hint of sweetness. Strain once to remove the almond granules.
2. It can be stored safely for 3 to 4 days in the refrigerator.

3) Cashew Milk

Cashews contain no cholesterol (like cow's milk) and are a good source of magnesium, phosphorus, manganese, copper, and iron.

SERVES 4

Ingredients

½ cup of cashews

2 cups of water

Method

1. Blend the cashews with the water till it's mixed well.

2. If you find it grainy, then strain the liquid.

GRAIN RECIPES

1) Katrina's Yummy Brown Rice Porridge

SERVES 1

Ingredients

½ cup of leftover brown rice (make sure you have brown rice in your fridge to make this the next morning)

¼ cup water or almond milk (don't use nuts if you are using almond milk)

1 tbs of mounaka raisins

½ apple cut into four, and sliced thin and long

1 tbs walnuts, roasted and chopped

1 tbs almonds, roasted and chopped

Dash of cinnamon

Method

1. Blend cooked (leftover) brown rice with water or almond milk. Keep it grainy.
2. In the meantime, stew the apples on low flame with a little water and cinnamon, and keep it covered.
3. Put brown rice in a porridge bowl, layer with apples, add mounaka raisins, and top it with nuts.

2) Basic Brown Rice

SERVES 2

Ingredients

1 cup brown rice (short grain)
2 cups of water
Pinch of sea salt
¼ tsp of lime juice (optional)

Method

1. Measure the grain and clean if required. Rinse in cold water.
2. Soak it for 1 to 8 hours, which will soften it, making it more digestible as well as eliminating the phytic acid. You can also add the lime juice here (optional).
3. Strain the water and add fresh water and bring to a boil.
4. Add a pinch of sea salt to help in the cooking process.

5. After the first boil, reduce heat, cover, and let it cook on a low flame for 35 to 40 minutes. Adding a tava (cast iron pan or flame deflector) after the first boil helps in cooking process.

Variation

You can use the same method and pressure cook your grain. But just remember, pressure cooking is yang compared to boiling. If you are going to pressure cook your beans, then boil your grain and vice versa—use both cooking styles at a given meal.

Note#: Never overcook a whole grain, as it gets converted to simple carbohydrates with a high glycemic load.

3) Brown Rice Salad

Makes for a great meal to carry to work or when you are on the run, as it can be had cold.

SERVES 4

Ingredients

2 cups of cooked brown rice

3 cups boiling water

1 small onion, diced

6 green beans, cut diagonally

1 cup cabbage, finely chopped

1 cup carrot, cut into small cubes

4 tbs sunflower seeds (optional)

Method

1. Add beans, carrot, and onion to boiling water. Do not over boil as they should be crisp.
2. Retain water as you lift the vegetables out with a strainer.
3. Blanch cabbage in the same water just for 1 minute.
4. Mix all the other ingredients and use a basic vinaigrette dressing.
5. The remaining water can be used as a broth in a soup.

Basic Vinaigrette Dressing

Makes 1½ cups

Ingredients

2 small garlic cloves, peeled and finely chopped

2 pinches of sea salt

⅓ cup lemon juice

1 to 3 madras onions (shallots), minced

Freshly ground black pepper

1 cup extra virgin olive oil or any of the other oils recommended in this book.

Method

1. Add all ingredients except oil in a small mixie jar and whisk together.
2. Slowly pour the olive oil in a steady stream This will make your dressing creamy.

3. Taste to adjust seasoning.

4. You can store this in the refrigerator for two meals.

4) Brown Rice Cutlets

This recipe is a great way to introduce brown rice to people who are just starting with it and even to kids.

Makes 6 cutlets

Ingredients

3 cups of cooked basic brown rice

1 carrot, grated

1 onion, finely chopped

3 cloves of garlic, finely chopped

3 tbs black sesame seeds, roasted

½ cup whole grain breadcrumbs

½ cup coriander leaves

Sea salt, a little chilli powder, or black pepper powder to taste

1 tbs extra virgin olive oil

Method

1. Sauté carrot, onion, and garlic in a pan on a low fire and cover for 5 minutes.

2. Take it off the fire and mix in the rice.

3. Shape into eight small (or six large) cutlets (you can wet your hands with water while doing this).

4. Roll over breadcrumbs and black sesame seeds on a plate so they are coated on both sides.

5. Pan fry in a shallow dish or bake at 150 degrees Celsius for 40 minutes on an oiled foil sheet.

5) Brown Rice with Leafy Greens

Adding green vegetables to your brown rice gives you a boost of Vitamin A, energizes your immune system, and helps to reduce anaemia.

SERVES 3

Ingredients

1 onion, thinly sliced

3 tbs of sesame or olive oil (dark sesame oil makes this taste better)

5 green onions, sliced diagonally

¾ kg of mixed greens. You can use spinach, cabbage, pak choi, fenugreek, or arugula

3 cups brown rice, cooked

1 tsp grated lemon zest and lemon juice

1 tsp ginger, grated

2 garlic cloves, finely chopped

Pinch of sea salt

Method

1. In a pan, sauté onion, garlic, and green onions. Add salt once they sizzle.

2. Add ginger and greens and sauté for a few minutes.

3. Add lemon juice and zest.

4. Add some water and then the rice. Mix well.
5. Cover the pan for about 5 minutes.

VEGETABLE RECIPES

1) Nishime

Nishime literally means 'waterless cooking'; the vegetables cook in their own juices. The mechanics of this style works like a steam engine in the body, providing it with steady energy in the abdomen region. It also stabilizes blood sugar levels. I often employ this cooking technique while making dishes for Katrina . Use this style two to three times a week for any meal.

Serves Nishime-style vegetables

Ingredients

1 carrot, cut into cubes

¼ cabbage, cut into wedges

1 onion, cut into wedges

¼ cup squash, cut into wedges or cubed

2 to 3 inch strips of kombu (optional)

Method

1. Place kombu at the bottom of a heavy cast iron pot (creuset).
2. Layer vegetables on top of each other and add ½ inch water.

3. Cover pot and bring to a boil over medium flame. Then lower flame and cook for 20 minutes. If water evaporates, add more.

4. When vegetables get tender, add a few drops of soy sauce, ginger juice, or any other seasoning of your choice.

5. Cover for 5 minutes

6. Remove from gas and let it sit for 5 minutes before serving.

2) Vegetable Stock

Makes 12 cups

Ingredients

4 celery stalks, chopped

2 onions, diced

4 cloves of garlic, peeled and finely chopped

3 to 4 carrots, cubed

2 cup mushrooms, chopped

Handful of parsley

4 bay leaves (tej patta)

Pinch of sea salt

16 cups of water

Method

1. Add onions, garlic, and sea salt in a large vessel with 1 cup of water. After the first boil, let it simmer for about 10 minutes on medium flame.

2. Then add the remaining vegetables and water and bring to a boil.

3. Reduce heat and cook on a low fire for about 1 hour. The liquid should boil down to 12 cups.

4. Run water through a sieve, press down vegetables to squeeze out water. You can either discard the vegetables or use them in a soup.

Note#: You can use this stock in your soups, some vegetable curries, and some cold vegetable drinks as well.

3) Red Pumpkin (bhopla) Sautéed with Garlic and Basil

A simple, delicious, and quick recipe. This recipe is two pronged as it gives you upward energy if you stir fry it in the warm summer months. The energy, however, changes to inward if you bake it in winter.

SERVES 4

Ingredients

½ kg of red pumpkin, cubed

7 cloves of garlic, minced

2 tsp of dry basil

2 tbs of olive oil

Pinch of sea salt

Method

a. Stir fried

1. Boil pumpkin in water beforehand.

2. Add oil to a pan but do not heat to a very high temperature.

3. Add garlic and basil; when it sizzles, add sea salt. Sauté for 5 to 7 minutes. Do not let it burn.

4. Add pumpkin to this mix, and stir fry on high flame, tossing it till it is coated with basil and garlic.

b. Baked

1. Parboil the pumpkin.

2. Mix the oil, garlic, and herbs, and coat each piece with this mix.

3. Bake in the oven at 150 degrees celsius for 20 minutes.

4. Serve with arugula leaves.

4) Pumpkin Seed and Cashew Gravy

This gravy can be used with carrots or even with tofu. It makes for a nice thick sauce with noodles without any dairy or cream.

SERVES 6

Ingredients

¾ cup pumpkin seeds (magaj)

1 cup cashews (unsalted)

4 cups vegetable stock

4 tomatoes, chopped

2 to 3 cloves

2-inch stick of cinnamon

1½ inch piece ginger, grated

½ tsp turmeric, red chilli powder, coriander powder

Sea salt to taste

Method

1. In a pot, mix everything together and add stock.
2. After the first boil, simmer for half hour on low flame.
3. After it cools, blend mixture with hand blender.
4. Check the consistency. Add more vegetable stock if you want to thin it down.

5) Cauliflower with Cumin Lemon Scented Oil

Makes ½ cup of oil to toss cauliflower

Ingredients

½ cup olive oil

Grated zest of 1 lemon

1 tsp of cumin seeds

½ tsp of chilli flakes

½ tsp of sea salt

1 head of cauliflower

4 sprigs of basil, shredded

Method

To make the oil:

1. Place all the ingredients in a saucepan and cook over a low flame uncovered for 10 to 12 minutes.

2. Turn off the heat and let it stand undisturbed for 1 hour.
3. Strain the oil and reserve ¼ cup. Store the oil in a glass bottle. Seal it airtight. Refrigerate oil and use within 5 days.

To make the cauliflower:

4. In a pot, add water and boil cauliflower with a pinch of sea salt.
5. Drain and transfer to a serving bowl; allow it to cool.
6. Toss the cauliflower with the ¼ cup oil that was reserved.

6) Mushroom Moussaka with Tofu or Eggplant

SERVES 6

Ingredients

225g tofu or 2 eggplants, quartered
2 tbs olive oil
2 cups onions, chopped
½ kg mushrooms, chopped
1½ cups tomatoes, chopped
½ cup tomato paste
1 tsp cinnamon
Sea salt to taste
1 tsp of basil
1 cup parsley, chopped

Method

1. Heat olive oil in a deep saucepan or a wok.
2. Add onions, and cook over medium heat. When they sizzle and turn transluscent, add sea salt and stir for 10 minutes till the onions are done, but don't turn brown.
3. Add mushrooms and garlic, cover and lower flame. The mushrooms will take 5 to 7 minutes to cook.
4. Add tomatoes and the paste and all the dry seasonings, bring to a boil. Let it simmer for another 15 minutes.
5. When it's done, you can use a hand blender to blend this mix, as this gives it a nice texture.

To add tofu: Cut the tofu into cubes (medium) and add to the mushroom moussaka gravy, for the last 5 minutes.

To add eggplant: Salt them and set aside for 30 minutes (this will take away the bitter flavour or use as is). Oil a baking sheet, spread the eggplant, and bake till tender or for about 30 minutes at 180 degrees celsius. Alternatively, you can shallow fry them in a good oil like extra virgin olive, or high heat safflower. Add to the moussaka gravy.

Variation

Grease an oven-proof casserole dish with olive oil. You can layer this dish with eggplants first (at bottom), next bake the mushroom sauce, and keep layering in this fashion. Top it with bread crumbs and bake at approximately 180 degrees Celsius for 30 to 40 minutes.

7) Garlic French Beans

SERVES 6

Ingredients

1 head of garlic

1 kg of green beans, leave whole, boil in water for 5 minutes

2 tbs extra virgin olive oil

Sea salt to taste

2 tbs chilli flakes

2 tbs of water

Method

1. Preheat oven to 200 degrees Celsius. Place the entire head of garlic in a foil and drizzle some olive oil over it, cover it with foil, and leave it in the oven for about 1 hour.

2. After it's done (when tender), set aside to cool.

3. Remove garlic pulp from skins and set aside.

4. Add 3 tbs of oil to a warm skillet. Then add the garlic pulp and water and make a paste. Add sea salt and the chilli flakes.

5. Cook, stirring frequently.

6. Add the green beans and cook for 1 to 2 minutes.

8) Cabbage in Coriander Sauce

SERVES 4

Ingredients

For cabbage

- ½ head of cabbage, cut into thin long strips
- ½ cup coriander leaves
- 2 green chillies made into a paste (use 1 green chilly if you cannot handle spices)
- 3 tsp wheat flour (use sorghum if you are gluten intolerant)
- 2 tsp olive oil
- 2 cups soy milk (unsweetened)
- 1 tomato, finely sliced
- 2 tsp bread crumbs

For sauce

- 2 to 3 pods of garlic, minced
- 2 tsp ginger, minced
- 1 small bundle of coriander leaves
- 1 to 2 green chillies, minced
- 1½ cup coconut, grated
- 1½ tsp cumin powder
- 3 tsp coriander powder
- ½ tsp carom seeds (ajwain)
- ½ tsp fenugreek seeds (methi)
- ¼ to ½ cup vegetable stock

Method

1. Blend the ingredients for sauce in a blender. Use vegetable stock to help in the blending process.
2. Add the flour to a warm skillet. Then add soy milk, and green chilli paste, stirring constantly to make a paste. You should be able to coat the back portion of your stirring spoon, and see that the liquid does not slide off easily.
3. Add the green sauce and cook for about 10 minutes. After the first boil, lower the flame.
4. Add cabbage and cook for 5 to 6 minutes. Then add some sea salt.
5. Garnish with tomatoes, and then cook for 2 to 3 minutes more.

Variation

Alternatively, if you want to break it, put the cabbage in green sauce in a baking dish, grate tofu on top of the dish, and sprinkle bread crumbs on top. Bake for 20 minutes at 150 degrees Celsius for 10 to 15 minutes.

LEGUMES/BEANS

1) Green Moong Salad

SERVES 4

Ingredients

   1 large carrot, grated

½ green apple, chopped after deseeding

¼ cup green moong, cleaned, rinsed, and soaked overnight

1 tsp grated ginger

1 red bell pepper, roasted, skinned, and chopped

2 tbs lime juice

1 tbs olive oil

1 small green chilli, deseeded and choped

½ tsp mustard seeds

Sea salt to taste

Handful of coriander leaves

Method

1. Cook the beans and keep aside.
2. Once cooled, add carrot, apple, bell pepper, lemon juice, and ginger to the beans.
3. Heat oil and add mustard seeds. Cover till mustard seeds crackle, then add green chilli. Add this to the green moong mixture.
4. Mix in the coriander leaves and salt.

2) Chickpea with Leafy Greens

SERVES 4

Ingredients

2 tbs olive oil

4 to 5 garlic pods

2 medium onions, chopped

½ tsp cumin powder (jeera)

1 bunch of leafy greens (pak choi, spinach, or mustard leaves)

1 tsp of curry powder

½ tsp of ginger, grated

½ tsp of coriander powder (dhaniya)

¼ tsp chilli powder

1 cup vegetable stock

1½ cup chickpeas, cooked

1¼ cup tomatoes, cubed

Sea salt to taste

Method

1. Add oil to a cooking pot. Then add the onions and garlic and sauté for 2 to 3 minutes.

2. The moment the onions start to turn transluscent, add some salt and cumin powder. Cook for 5 minutes, stirring frequently.

3. Add the greens, cook for 5 minutes. Then add the curry powder, ginger, coriander powder, chilli powder, and vegetable stock

4. Bring to a boil, reduce flame, and add the chickpeas and tomatoes. Cook for 15 minutes, stirring constantly.

3) White Soybean Salad

SERVES 6

Ingredients

1½ cup white soybeans or a mix of white and black soybeans, soaked overnight, and pressure cooked the next morning, and drained once done

¼ cup dill (suha)

¼ cup tofu mayonnaise (see recipe on p 286)

½ cup parsley, minced

2 garlic pods

2 green onions, finely chopped, sideways

1 cucumber, cubed (small)

1 carrot, cubed (small)

½ red bell pepper, cubed (small)

Method

Combine all the ingredients together, and voila, it's ready!

4) White Beans (Kidney or Chawli) in Tomato Base

SERVES 4

Ingredients

1 tbs extra virgin olive oil

6 madras onions, chopped fine

1 tsp basil

½ tsp chilli powder

1½ cups white beans, pressure cooked

1 ½ cups tomatoes, diced (I like to boil them and skin them before use)

2 cups vegetable stock

Sea salt and freshly ground pepper to taste

Coriander or parsley leaves to garnish

Method

1. Heat oil and add madras onions. Cover and cook for 5 minutes.

2. Add garlic, basil, and chilli powder and sauté for 2 minutes.

3. Add tomatoes and cook till semi done.

4. Add beans and vegetable stock.

5. Cover and cook for about 10 minutes.

6. Add salt and pepper.

7. Add garnish.

5) Red Kidney Bean Cutlets

SERVES 4

Ingredients

1½ cups red kidney beans, cooked

½ cup brown rice, cooked

1 onion, chopped

1 red bell pepper, roasted, skinned, and finely chopped

½ cup chopped celery

2 garlic pods, finely chopped

2 tbs of extra virgin or any other oil

½ tsp chilli powder

½ tsp dried thyme or any other herb you would use for seasoning

Sea salt and freshly ground black pepper to taste

1 tbs parsley or coriander leaves

Method

1. Heat oil and add all the vegetables starting with onion and garlic, and then add the dry herbs, and sea salt and pepper. Stir occasionally and keep it covered to let it cook in its own juices for about 10 minutes.

2. After 10 minutes, take it off the heat and let it cool.

3. Once cooled, add the brown rice and kidney beans and blend in a food processor.

4. Shape into cutlets and pan fry.

6) Black Kidney Bean Salad

This salad is simple yet super delicious. You can even use red kidney beans or any other whole beans.

SERVES 4

Ingredients

1 cup dried black beans or any other whole bean

1 red bell pepper, roasted over an open flame, peeled, seeded, and diced

2 to 3 celery stalks, diced or handful parsley

1 onion, diced

¼ cup fresh parsley, minced

Zest of 1 lemon, grated

4–5 dates, deseeded and chopped

Variation

As we don't get good quality vinegar in the market, I use lime juice instead, and stevia instead of other sweeteners.

For dressing

1/3 cup extra virgin olive oil

1 tsp soy sauce

2 tsp lemon juice

3 tbs balsamic vinegar

2 tsp stevia

2 garlic pods, minced

Juice of 1 lemon

Juice of 1 orange (optional)

Method

1. Warm oil in a pan over a low flame. Add soy sauce and cook for 3 to 4 minutes.
2. In a small bowl, whisk together all the ingredients for dressing.

3. Mix beans with vegetables and pour in the dressing.
4. Serve warm or chilled.

GOOD FERMENTED FOODS

1) Pressed Salad

This salad is highly recommended for people who were, or still are, non vegetarian, as it breaks down the saturated fat from animal food. It is also beneficial for people who are leading pressured lives, as it releases tension. I use it for clients suffering from chronic fatigue and fibromyalgia, a condition of tender points of pain in the shoulder (this area reflects the small intestine). This salad makes them flexible. Pressed salad will help to assimilate your entire meal and provide you with good bacteria. You can even save some and have it the next day with another meal.

SERVES 4

Ingredients

½ cup cucumber, sliced

½ cup cabbage, sliced

½ cup white radish (mooli)

¼ cup celery

¼ cup red onion

1 tsp salt

Tip#: Green apples, when in season, make this salad nice and tangy.

Method

1. Mix all vegetables with sea salt in a large bowl, and gently press and massage with fingers (like you are making atta for rotis) until they wilt.
2. Place a plate on top of the vegetables and press down with a heavy weight. I usually have a brick wrapped in a clean cloth handy.
3. Allow to stand with pressure on top for 45 minutes and let water release from the vegetables.
4. Discard the water and rinse with fresh filter water and eat as a side dish.
5. Use different coloured veggies and throw in a green like celery. Add a little chilli powder before eating (like a kimchi) for a hint of spice, or add a dash of ground peanuts.

2) Sauerkraut

Sauerkraut means 'sour cabbage' in German. It's basically shredded cabbage fermented with lactic acid bacteria, and once made, it can be kept for months (like our Indian pickles). In cold weather, it is good to eat even without refrigeration. An excellent side dish to regenerate your digestive system, it brings your digestion back to balance (acid-alkaline), gives you lactobacillus acidophilus or good bacteria which balances secretions in your stomach, gives you the right enzymes, vitamins, strengthens spleen and pancreas, and improves digestion, especially of fats which we Indians consume a lot. I recommend it with meals 3 to 4 times a week. Especially beneficial for people with candida, cancer, degenerative conditions such as cancer, thyroid, irritable bowel disorder with Crohn's disease, and low immunity.

Makes ½ a jar of sauerkraut

Ingredients

You will need a substantial amount of vegetables. Use either cabbage or a mix of beetroot, cabbage, cauliflower, white radish, cucumbers, and carrots. (sometimes I add green apples). Start with a total of 2 kgs of all the vegetables.

3 tbs sea salt

A large and deep bowl. Preferably a crock pot.

Method

1. Finely chop all vegetables.
2. Sprinkle salt on the vegetables, as you keep layering the pot—the salt keeps the vegetables crunchy, and pulls water out of them; this makes the brine for this dish. If it is very hot then you can use more salt.
3. Mix well and pack it down in the deep bowl.
4. Cover the pot with a tight-fitting lid, pressing vegetables in, and place a weight on top. Wait for the water to rise up to the lid.
5. Check the water level every few hours and keep pressing the lid further down. Continue the process for a whole day. If the brine does not rise to the lid, make additional salt water (1 tbs to 250 ml of water;

stir till all the salt is dissolved before adding more)
and add to the jar.

6. Leave it to ferment in a room with air for 5 to 7 days.
    Discard any old moldy vegetables on top. After the
    fermentation process, put the remaining mixture in
    a glass jar with a lid and refrigerate. This can be used
    for 4 to 8 months.

3) Quick Sweet and Sour Lime pickle

Makes ½ a bottle

Ingredients

6 limes
4 crushed cardamoms
12 whole cloves
1 tbs sea salt
2 tbs cumin seeds
Lime juice (about 6 tbs)
Chilli powder to taste

Method

1. Cut each lime into 4 pieces.
2. Sprinkle with dry masalas.
3. Put in a glass jar and pour lime juice over it.
4. Cover with a muslin cloth and keep tightly covered
    in a warm place for up to 1 week.
5. Pick up jar and move around in a swirling motion
    daily.

6. Ready after 1 week. Refrigerate.

4) Fruit Kimchi

This is a great recipe as we Indians love our fruit.

Makes 2 cups

Ingredients

2 pears or apples, cubed with skin

A bunch of grapes, deseeded and cut in half

Less than half a pineapple, cubed

2 tsp sea salt

Juice of 1 lemon (optional)

Coriander powder

Red or green chillies, finely chopped

Garlic pods and 2-inch piece of ginger as per taste

Walnuts, almonds, dates, or sesame seeds (optional)

Method

1. Mix everything , add sea salt and lime juice.
2. Put in a deep bowl, cover with lid and press it down with a weight.
3. Keep for a few hours or overnight.

5) White Radish (Mooli) and Lemon Quick Pickle

Makes ½ a bottle

Ingredients

1 large white radish (mooli), cut in thin round slices or
finger sizes

Zest of 1 lemon

½ to 1 tbs sea salt

Method

1. Massage the sea salt into the radish until it releases
   water.
2. Mix in lemon zest.
3. Put in a bowl and press it down with a lid.
4. Store in a cool place for 1 to 2 days.
5. Remove lid and store in a glass jar in fridge.
6. Use small amount with meals.
7. Rinse with water if it is too salty before eating.

SPREADS/SNACKS/SAUCES

Healthy Spreads

1) Hearty Hummus

Get the necessary calcium and vitamins from this dish.

SERVES 4

Ingredients

1 cup chickpeas, soaked overnight and pressure
cooked.

Health tip #1: Cook with a stamp-sized piece of kombu if possible to get your trace minerals.
Health tip #2: Save the chickpea liquid and use some to blend it in mixer.

1 or 2 garlic pods

Juice of 1 lemon

2 tbs tahini or toasted and ground sesame seeds

Sea salt to taste. If using kombu, pull back on the sea salt

1 tbs parsley or green onion to garnish

Variation to make it spicy

4 dry red chillies, deseeded

1½ tsp cumin

1 red bell pepper, roasted, skinned, and finely chopped

3 sundried tomatoes

¼ cup chopped coriander leaves

Method

1. Steam or sauté garlic and keep it aside.
2. Combine all the ingredients, except the green onion, in a mixer (use blender blade); use bean liquid to blend to a paste.
3. Garnish with parsley or green onion.

2) Creamy Vegan Tofu Mayonnaise

Get your protein without the saturated fat and digestive enzymes.

SERVES 6

Ingredients

- 1 pack of mori-nu silken tofu or any other tofu with a creamy consistency. You may need to add soy milk to get this.
- 2 tbs lemon juice
- 1 tbs miso (white)
- 2 tsp of olive oil

Method

1. Steam tofu in a steamer for 3–5 minutes and let it cool a bit.
2. Add all the ingredients to your blender and mix together.

Variation

Sometimes I add 1 tsp of mustard to give it a twist. This also benefits your liver.

3) Wholesome Bean Spread

Lower your cholesterol when you snack and keep your blood sugar stable with this spread.

SERVES 6

Ingredients

2 cups of leftover beans or lentils

1 stalk of a green onion, finely chopped

2 stalks of celery, finely chopped

Some parsley, finely chopped

1 tbs lemon juice

Sea salt to taste

¼ cup roasted sesame seeds (or any seed)

Method

1. Make sure the beans do not have too much water. So if it's a dal, then keep some water to blend since we are making a paste.

2. You can use a fork to mash the ingredients together or put it in a blender to mix it well.

3. Use on crackers, bread, or rotis.

4) Smooth and Sweet Veggie Carrot Butter

Get all the Vitamin A you need for the day; look younger.

SERVES 6

Ingredients

4 cups of carrots, cubed

1 tbs arrowroot powder—dissolve in ¼ cup water

2 tbs tahini (sesame butter) or roasted and ground
sesame seeds

¼ cup water

Sea salt to taste

Method

1. Boil carrots and add a pinch of salt, then let it cool.
2. Add this to a blender. Use some liquid (could use
   the liquid you have used to boil the carrots).
3. Mix in the arrowroot liquid and put the blend on the
   gas to heat.
4. Keep stirring, as the arrowroot thickens it a bit.
5. Add the tahini or ground sesame seeds; tahini usually
   works better here.

SNACKS

1) Sweet Potato Pancakes

The great thing about this snack is that you can make it for
breakfast, as a snack in the evening with chutney, or even
as a component to your dinner meal, if you keep off grain
in the evening. It's a high-starch snack, excellent for people

who run low on serotonin. Besides, sweet potatoes have a low glycemic index and will keep your sugar levels steady.

SERVES 4

Ingredients

3 cups sweet potato, grated

3 tbs lemon juice

¼ cup onion, grated

Salt and black pepper to taste

2 tbs of flour to bind (I use sorghum)

Method

1. Mix all the ingredients well.
2. Line your pan with oil (I use a spray olive).
3. Take some potato mix in your hand and flatten it in your palm like a pancake—it does not have to be too tightly packed.
4. Put in on your pan, and pat the pancake down.
5. Shallow fry on one side. Once lightly brown, flip over.
6. Serve warm with chutney.

2) Foxtail Millet or any Whole Grain Millet Poha

This grain nourishes your spleen/pancreas/stomach, so it is excellent for diabetics and anyone with a blood sugar problem. It also aids digestion. Your stomach has to have strength to digest your food; your spleen must extract the lipids (fats) from that food and convert them into energy for the body; your pancreas needs to release digestive enzymes to help breakdown the fats, proteins, and carbohydrates. Millet is one grain that achieves all of this smoothly. It's gluten free, high in iron, manganese, phosphorus, B and E Vitamins, and most of all, tryptophan. So while it repairs your heart, spleen, and pancreas, it also provides you energy, repairs body tissue, and also rids the body of acid toxins. I use foxtail millet—cheena, a whole yellow grain.

SERVES 4
Cooking the millet for the poha

Ingredients

1 cup of millet
3 cups of water
Pinch of sea salt

Method

1. Clean the millet and wash it. I usually use a small strainer.
2. For a lovely texture, dry roast it in a pan (medium heat), till it releases a nutty aroma. Do not brown.
3. Bring water to a boil. Add a pinch of sea salt and millet.
4. Turn it down to low flame after the first boil.
5. Cover and let it simmer for 20 minutes. The millet will absorb the water and soften.

Cooking the Poha

Ingredients

1 cup dry millet, cooked

Curry leaves

Boiled peas

½ sweet potato, cubed (boiled)

1 carrot, cubed (boiled)

Mustard seeds

1 onion, chopped

Coriander leaves to garnish

¼ tsp red chilli powder

1 tsp sesame oil

½ tsp coriander powder

½ tsp turmeric powder

Salt to taste

Method

1. Take 1 tsp sesame oil in a pan.
2. Add the mustard seeds and curry leaves.
3. Once the seeds pop, add the onions.
4. Sauté for 5 minutes. Do not brown completely.
5. Add the millet and veggies.
6. Toss to coat with onions, mustard, and curry leaves
7. Add dry spices.
8. Toss and mix well. Garnish with coriander leaves.
9. Serve with a dash of lime.

3) Crunchy Sauerkraut Snack

Get your digestive enzymes going while you snack with a crunch. You can always make a bottle over the weekend and keep it in the fridge at work.

SERVES 4

Ingredients

Leftover brown rice (optional)

Some sauerkraut

Any toasted seeds like sunflower, sesame

Method

1. Buys some crackers or crisp bread.
2. Mix all together (can omit the rice).
3. And lay it on the crisp bread or crackers with some chutney.

4) Mock Egg Tofu Salad

Great in a sandwich or on a crackers or by itself. Again can be used at breakfast to help you get over your egg consumption. While bringing in a great source of digestible protein and giving you Vitamin B, minerals, phosphorus, iron, sodium, potassium, and low calories, tofu also has the calcium content equal to that of milk.

SERVES 6

Ingredients

- 1 pack (225g) of silken mori-nu tofu or any other tofu
- 1 onion, grated
- 2 celery stalks, finely chopped
- 2 carrots, grated
- Sea salt to taste
- 1 tbs of white wine vinegar

Method

1. Steam the tofu (make sure all the water is squeezed out of your tofu block) and keep aside.
2. Mix all the ingredients and crumble tofu with your hand and mix well.
3. Chill the salad for 10 to 15 minutes before serving.

5) Gratifying Green Smoothie

Get your daily dose of greens. Makes for a great filler in between meals.

SERVES 2

Ingredients

- 1 banana (optional)
- 1 apple, chopped
- ½ cup water or vegetable stock
- 1 cup of sprouts
- 1 tbs spirulina powder
- 2 tsp lemon juice

1 tsp of wheat grass powder

4 tbs aloe vera juice

Method

1. Put the fruit and water/stock in a blender, and blend until smooth.

2. Add all other ingredients, and blend again until smooth.

3. Pour into glasses and enjoy.

6) Crispy Chopped Waldorf Chapati/Corn (Makai) Roti Wraps

SERVES 4 TO 6

Ingredients

½ cabbage head, shredded and chopped

1 green apple, cored and chopped into small cubes

1 stalk of celery, chopped

½ red onion, diced

½ cup toasted almonds, roughly chopped

½ cup mounaka raisins

1 tbs black sesame seeds

4 to 6 large whole wheat chapatis or corn (makai) rotis/ tortillas

For dressing

½ cup tofu mayonnaise

½ cup strained soy yoghurt

Juice of 1 large orange

Salt and pepper to taste

Method

1. In a small jar, combine the dressing ingredients and give everything a good shake. Set aside.
2. Combine the cabbage, apple, celery, and onion into a large bowl and toss well. Pour dressing over salad, add in the nuts, mounaka raisins, and sesame seeds and give everything a final toss.
3. Add a couple large spoonfuls (at least a cup or so) of the salad into the middle of the tortilla and roll tightly, like a burrito: bottom folds up first and then tightly wrap up the sides. Wrap in butter paper if you like to seal in the drips.
4. Or skip the wrap and just eat as a salad. It's delicious either way.

7) Cauliflower with Lemon Tahini Dressing

SERVES 2

Ingredients

1 head of cauliflower, medium-sized florets, boiled

For sauce

3 tbs tahini

2 tbs light miso (optional)

6 tbs water

1 tbs lemon juice (or to taste)

Method

1. Combine the sauce ingredients in a saucepan and place on low flame and slowly bring to a boil.
2. Stir frequently for about 1 minute, until sauce is thick.
3. Use immediately over boiled cauliflower.

SOUPS

1) Sweet Miso Soup

SERVES 12

Ingredients

8 cups water or vegetable stock

1 small squash/red pumpkin, cubed

1 medium onion, cut into thin rounds

1 small white radish, cut into thin rounds

6 tbs white or barley miso

1 green onion stalk, finely chopped

Handful of fresh parsley

Method

1. Bring 8 cups of water to a boil.
2. Add onion to the pot. Let it simmer uncovered for 5 minutes.

3. Add the radish and let it simmer for another 5 minutes.

4. Now add the squash and simmer for about 5 minutes or till tender. Remove from heat.

5. Place a small amount of the hot soup in a small bowl, add the miso, whisk till smooth, and return to pot.

6. Stir and garnish with green onions and parsley.

Note #: Do not boil soup again after adding Miso as the beneficial microorganisms that aid digestion get killed.

2) My Mom's Broccoli Soup

Serves: 2 to 4

Ingredients

5 cups of water or vegetable stock (enhances nutrient value)

1½ cup broccoli, chopped

1 small onion, finely chopped

½ sweet potato, cubed

1½ cup brown rice, cooked

2 tbs miso. Always use a lighter miso for children as the darker versions have a stronger taste

Method

1. Bring water, broccoli, sweet potato, and onion to a boil (or pressure cook); you can also use vegetable stock.

2. Cover and let it simmer for 10 minutes.

3. After the vegetables are tender, cool the liquid, mix in the brown rice, and put it in a blender or use a hand blender.

4. Mix 1 to 2 tsp of miso in the soup (by mixing separately in a cup and adding to soup).

5. Garnish with chopped broccoli.

Variation

You can use celery or lettuce instead of broccoli.

3) Fresh Corn Chowder Soup

Makes 6 cups

Ingredients

1 onion, diced

2 medium celery stalks, finely chopped

6 corn cobs, shelled

1 large sweet potato, cubed

4 cups vegetable stock or water

3 tbs of light miso

Method

1. Place in a pot the onion, celery stalks, corn, and sweet potatoes and pour in the stock or water.

2. Bring to a boil; reduce heat and let it simmer for 10 to 15 minutes covered, till potatoes are tender.

3. Add 1½ tsp salt and ½ tsp black pepper and let it simmer for 5 more minutes. Blend in a mixer after it cools and return to heat for one more boil.
4. Add 3 tbs of light miso.
5. Garnish with parsley or coriander.

4) Round Vegetable Soup

For tremendous calming energy and a satisfied feeling in your belly.

SERVINGS: 4

Ingredients

½ cup yam (suran), cubed

2 turnips, cubed

3 to 4 colocasia (arbi), diced

2 carrots, diced

1 white radish, diced

1 onion, finely sliced

3 to 4 cinnamon sticks

3 to 4 cloves

1 tbs curry powder

4 tsp dark or light miso

1 tbs olive oil

3 cups of water or vegetable stock

Method

1. Add oil to a pot before it heats up. Then add onions, cinnamon, and cloves. Sauté till onions are a little soft.

2. Add vegetables in the following order: turnips, yam, colocasia, white radish, and carrots. Sauté for 10 minutes and then add the curry powder.

3. Add water or stock and after first boil, let it simmer on low flame for 20 minutes.

4. Once the vegetables are tender, blend them with a hand blender.

5. Take out a little soup in a cup, add the miso, mix well, and put it back into the soup pot. Give it a good stir.

6. Garnish with parsley.

5) Bohemian Soup

SERVES 4 TO 5

Ingredients

1½ cup chickpeas, cooked

2 medium tomatoes

2 cups of onions, diced

2 tbs olive oil

3 to 4 garlic cloves, minced

2 cups sweet potato, peeled and cut into cubes

1 stalk of celery, finely chopped

1 tsp sea salt

2 tsp chilli powder

1 tsp turmeric

1 tsp basil

Pinch of cinnamon

1 green bell pepper, chopped

3 cups of water

Method

1. Blanch tomatoes in boiling water for 1 minute and remove the skin after taking out from water. Chop and remove the seeds.

2. Heat olive oil and add onions and garlic; sauté for 5 minutes till onions are translucent.

3. Add turmeric, chilly powder, basil, cinnamon, and sea salt. Add water, cover, and cook for 20 minutes.

4. Add tomatoes, green bell pepper, and chickpeas. Cook covered for 10 to 15 minutes.

6) Cauliflower Soup

SERVES 4

Ingredients

½ onion, cubed

2½ cups of cauliflower, cut into medium-sized pieces

½ tsp olive oil

1½ cups of water, boiled.

1 tbs light miso (optional).

½ stalk green onion, side cut, for garnishing.

½ red bell pepper (optional), roasted, skinned, and diced.

Method

1. Heat oil and add onions, sauté for 5 minutes.
2. Add cauliflower, sauté for 5 minutes.
3. Add the water, cover and let it simmer for about 10 minutes, till cauliflower gets done.
4. Transfer the soup to a blender and add water if required.
5. Return to the pan you were cooking soup in, and cook on a slow flame for 3 to 4 more minutes.
6. Garnish with red bell peppers and green onions.

7) Tomato Shorba

SERVES 2

Ingredients

2 tomatoes

1 tsp gram flour (besan)

1 tsp coconut milk

1 tsp cumin seeds (jeera)

5 curry leaves

Sea salt to taste

½ tsp lime juice

Coriander leaves for garnishing

Method

1. Plunge tomatoes in hot water, remove skin, deseed, and finely chop.
2. First dissolve gram flour in coconut milk, then blend in a blender.
3. Add oil to a pan and warm it, then add cumin seeds and curry leaves. Sauté for 1 to 2 minutes.
4. Add the tomatoes and sauté for 3 to 4 minutes.
5. Add the coconut milk,, sea salt and boil, let it simmer for 3 to 4 minutes after first boil.
6. Garnish with coriander leaves.

JUICES

1) The Pimple Cure

SERVES 2

Ingredients

6 carrots
½ green capsicum
lime juice (optional)

Method

1. Chop carrots and capsicum and process in a mixer and add some water.
2. You can add some lime juice.

2) The Complete Cleanser

SERVES 2

Ingredients

½ cucumber

½ beetroot

3 carrots

Method

1. Finely chop all vegetables and process in a mixer and add some water.
2. Add some lime.

3) The Alkalizer

SERVES 2

Ingredients

3 stalks of celery

2 carrots

2 inch piece of cabbage

Method

1. Finely chop all the veggies and process in a mixer and add some water.
2. Add some lime at the end.

Avoid if you have a thyroid condition

4) The Hair Tonic

SERVES 2

Ingredients

6 leaves of spinach
Alfalfa sprouts
4 carrots

Method

1. Chop the carrots.
2. Process all the veggies in a mixer and add some water.

5) The Nifty Nail Blend

SERVES 2

Ingredients

4 to 5 spinach leaves
½ green capsicum
4 carrots
1 cucumber

Method

1. Chop cucumber, capsicum, and carrots. Process all the veggies in a mixer and add some water.

HOME REMEDIES

1) Sweet Vegetable Drink

Relaxes the stomach and muscles, and curtails sweet cravings.

SERVES 2

Method

1. Finely chop equal amounts of four vegetables— onions, carrots, cabbage, and sweet squash (bhopla).
2. Boil four times the amount of water and throw the veggies in. Boil for 2 to 3 minutes. Reduce flame to low, cover, and let it simmer for 20 minutes.
3. Strain the vegetables from the broth. Don't throw away the veggies; you can use them later in soups or stews.
4. Drink the broth either hot or at room temperature.

2) Liver Flush Remedy

SERVES 2

Ingredients

¼ cup white radish (mooli)

½ cup radish or turnip greens (top part of the radish or turnip)

¼ cup green onions

¼ cup sprouts (preferably alfalfa)

¼ cup (about 2) shiitake mushrooms

Method

1. Chop all vegetables.
2. Add 5 cups of water, bring to a boil, then lower the flame and simmer for about 30 minutes.
3. Strain the water and drink the liquid. You may have a glass leftover for one more day, which can be stored in your fridge and warmed and used the next day.
4. You can choose to supplement with the following: CoQ10, Vitamin A and E, green and white tea extracts. This is entirely optional, as I believe the foods will do just that as well.

3) Lung Remedy

SERVES 2

Ingredients

½ cup lotus root
Less than ½ cup radish leaves
Less than ½ cup carrot
1 dried shiitake mushroom, soaked and chopped

Method

1. Grate all the veggies.
2. Boil in 4 cups water for 15 to 20 minutes on a low flame.
3. After boiling, drink 1 cup of the juice.

4) Fresh Lotus Root Tea

SERVES 2

Ingredients

½ cup lotus root juice

½ cup water

Pinch of sea salt

Method

1. Grate lotus root and squeeze juice.
2. Place in a pot to boil.
3. Stir continuously and after first boil simmer for 3 to 4 minutes on a reduced flame.
4. Drink warm.

#Note: Both the above remedies are extremely helpful when you have chest congestion, a cold, or any other bronchial issue.

5) Carrot White Radish Drink

SERVES 2

Ingredients

½ cup grated carrot

½ cup grated white radish (mooli)

1½ cups water

Method

1. Place carrot, radish in water and bring to a boil
2. Simmer for 3 to 4 minutes
3. Drink vegetables and broth warm

6) Kidney remedy

SERVES 2

Ingredients

Kidney beans (black beans will do), soaked overnight
3 shiitake mushrooms, soaked
½ cup white radish, shredded

Method

1. Add white radish to the kidney beans and shiitake mushrooms.
2. Add 5 times the amount of water, boil and then lower flame for 25 minutes.
3. Drink 1 cup daily for 10 days.

7) Shiitake Mushroom Tea

Soak 1–2 mushrooms until tender. Place with 1 cup water in a pan, bring to a boil, lower gas for 15 minutes and simmer. Strain and drink warm.

DESSERTS

1) Baked Apple or Pears
Stuffed with walnuts and mounaka raisins

SERVES 4

Ingredients

2 apples or pears, cored
¼ cup mounaka raisins
½ cup walnuts, chopped
¼ tsp cinnamon
1 tsp stevia powder
¼ cup sugar-free apple juice

Method

1. Soak raisins in apple juice for 40 minutes.
2. Mix the walnuts, mounaka, stevia, and cinnamon.
3. Stuff the core with this mix.
4. Wrap each half in a foil.
5. Put in a baking tray and cover ½ inch of baking pan with apple juice.
6. Bake for 20 minutes.

Variation

You can just bake apples or pears and add some cinnamon, and sprinkle with raisins and nuts.

2) Almond Oatmeal Custard

SERVES 6

Ingredients

½ cup oats roasted in a pan

3 cups cooked oats

2 apples, grated

Sea salt (pinch)

1 tsp cinnamon

½ cup almonds, ground

⅓ tsp stevia powder

Method

1. Brush a pie pan with some oil.
2. Sprinkle the roasted oats at the bottom.
3. Mix the cooked oats, cinnamon, apples, sea salt, and stevia.
4. Fill up the pie pan with this mixture.
5. Sprinkle the ground almonds on top.
6. Bake for 30 minutes.
7. Cut into pie slices before serving.

   (Adapted from *Healing with Whole Foods* by Paul Pitchford)

3) Fruit Kanten (Great in warm weather)

SERVES 3

Ingredients

½ cup pears, steamed and puréed

½ cup strawberries, halved

2 tbs china grass

Pinch of sea salt

2 cups apple juice

Method

1. Put china grass in apple juice and bring to simmer, keep stirring (should not form lumps).
2. Take serving bowls, put puréed pear at bottom and arrange strawberries on top.
3. Pour china grass liquid on top of it.
4. This will take some time to set, after 15 to 20 minutes, put it in the fridge to chill.
5. Consume cold.

4) Cashewnut Cream (A perfect alternative to dairy cream)

Ingredients

1 cup cashews (unsalted)

1/3 tsp lemon rind (optional)

½ tsp vanilla essence

¾ cup water

2 tsp pure maple syrup or 1 tsp stevia powder

Method

1. Soak cashews in water for an hour and a half.
2. Place all the ingredients in a blender and purée till smooth.

5) Fig Cake

SERVES 12

Ingredients

1½ cups almond milk (see recipe on p 256)

3 cups barley (jov) flour or sorghum (jovar) for a gluten-free version

1½ tsp baking powder

¼ tsp sea salt

⅔ cup pure maple syrup

½ cup olive oil

⅔ cup orange juice

Zest of 1 orange

Zest of 2 limes

1 tsp vanilla essence

1 tbs lemon juice

2 cups cashew cream

Method

1. Preheat oven to 175 degrees Celsius.
2. Heat the almond milk and add figs to it, soak figs for 10 minutes to soften.
3. In a bowl, mix your dry ingredients.
4. Take the almond milk from soaking figs, and it should make 1 cup of milk, otherwise add some more to make a cup.
5. Blend wet ingredients together, add to dry ingredients, and blend with cake blender.
6. Fold figs into this batter.
7. Oil a cake tin, and transfer the batter to the tin.
8. Bake for 45 to 50 minutes at 175 degrees Celsius.
9. Allow cake to cool for 20 minutes and then turn it out on a cake rack, let it cool completely.
10. Cut individual slices, pour cashew cream on each slice (about ¼ cup).

(Adapted from *Sweet and Natural* by Meredith McCarthy)

6) Creamy Lemon Pie

Makes 1 pie

Ingredients

3 cups pineapple juice

⅛ tsp sea salt

¼ cup pure maple syrup

4 tbs arrowroot powder

1 tbs lemon juice

1 tsp lemon zest

⅔ cup cashews (unsalted)

Granola crust (see recipe)

Method

1. Blend cashews, pineapple juice, sea salt, maple syrup, arrowroot powder, and lemon juice in a blender.
2. Add to a pan and let simmer on slow gas until thick, and add lemon zest.
3. Pour into the granola crust.
4. Chill overnight, before serving.

7) Granola Crust for Pies

Ingredients

½ cup pure maple syrup

½ cup olive oil

¼ cup apple juice

½ tbs cinnamon powder

½ cup almond slices

1 tsp vanilla essence

3 cups oats

Method

1. Preheat oven to 170 degrees Celsius.
2. Combine all ingredients in a bowl.

3. Put it in a greased baking pan, bake for 20 minutes.
4. After it's done, cool it and break it up.
5. Use apple juice and oil to press it into the pan to form the base of your pie crust and use it for the sides as well.

CONDIMENTS

1) Gomashio

What is gomashio? This recipe combines sea salt and sesame seeds. The combination of oil and minerals from the salt help your blood condition to stay more alkaline and also gives you the calcium you require.

Ingredients

8 level tbs of sesame seeds (tan or black)
1½ tsp of sea salt

Method

1. Wash the sesame seeds in a strainer and allow water to drain.
2. Dry roast the sesame seeds on medium flame.
3. Transfer sea salt to a bowl in which you can pound them with your hand or with a pounding instrument (hand pounding grinder, preferably not mixer).
4. When seeds leave an aroma and start to pop, they are ready (keep stirring with a wooden spatula till this stage).

5. Add seeds to the grinder bowl, and start to pound, mix, and grind in a steady circular motion until it is 80 to 85 percent done.

6. Store in a glass jar, sprinkle ½ to 1 tsp on food.

2) Carrot Radish Condiment

SERVES 2

Ingredients

- 1 tbs of grated carrot
- 1 tbs of grated white radish

Have with meals for up to 5 times a week when on a weight loss plan.

Let's face it, beauty does get you places; but aren't we all looking for that everlasting beauty? The definition of beauty changes with time and age. So I hope that this book has not just helped you address more than what leads to being beautiful, but also provided you with tools to reach everlasting health and happiness to a really beautiful you. Cut through what the media bombards you with and know that you can achieve true beauty from 'outside in' with simple foods and the knowledge of how to use them. Carry more than just beauty with you as you go from one year to next; also carry the beautiful, spiritual, and emotional you. I hope I have given you all the tools to do so, and made it simple for you. Love yourself as you are, and look in the mirror everyday and appreciate at least one thing about yourself on this journey to a beautiful you. As Oprah once said, 'What you think you know in your 20s and 30s really comes alive in your 40s'. What you think makes you beautiful today, will change tomorrow and the day after. So grasp the 'real stuff' that makes you what you are.

SOURCE LIST

Conscious Foods

Phone Orders Only: 022 24974035; 022 24947902; 022 24934552; 022 24934551
   Also stocked at all major Nature's Basket Stores (by Godrej)
   Pulses, grains, snacks, and more

Navdanya Organics

No. 10, Mayfair Housing Society
   Off Andheri Link Road
   Andheri (West)
   Mumbai 400053
   Phone: 022 66790081; 9324288418
   Pulses, grains, spices, seeds, and more

The Altitude Store

16, Shanti Niketan Market

New Delhi 110021
www.thealtitudestore.com
Phone: 09811755222; 011 42705858
Natural sweeteners, pulses, grains, healthy organic snacks, natural oils

Naturally Yours

Shop No. 3, ground floor,
    Neelkanth Commercial Complex,
    Chembur Station Road,
    Next to Adarsh Hotel,
    Chembur East
    Mumbai, Maharashtra
    Phone: 022 32230003
    Organic vegetables, produce

Fab India Organics

Outlets all over India
    www.fabindia.com

Dakini Health Foods

Email: dakini@rediffail.com
    Phone: 020 32505101; 09890997610
    Sesame butter, sunflower butter, peanut butter, etc.

Soulfood by (Shonali Sabherwal)

www.soulfoodshonali.com
    Email: shonaalii@macrobioticsindia.com
    Phone: 09819035604

Products: Sugar, dairy, yeast, non GMO, gluten-free organic meals, snacks, and desserts

Kika

kikafoods@gmail.com
Phone: 9820397716 (Atika)
Blend of organic grain porridge

Nature's Basket

Outlets all over Mumbai and Delhi
www.naturesbasket.co.in

Mumbai
Phone (Bandra): 022 26425050; 022 26421122; (Oshiwara): 022 26300766; 022 26300714

Delhi
Ground floor M 54, M block GKII
Near bank of India
New Delhi
Phone: 011 40565891
Speciality foods, some organic

The Arya Vaidya Pharmacy India

136/137 Trichy Road
Ramnathapuram
Coimbatore 641045
Tamil Nadu
www.avpayurveda.com
Phone: 042 24322888; 042 2313188
Ayurvedic panchakarma products for beauty and health

ACKNOWLEDGEMENTS

I would first like to thank the Divine for bringing me to my true calling and my clients for believing and supporting me in my work.

My editor, Milee—I am glad we found each other. Thank you for supporting this book and my larger vision of bringing macrobiotics to India.

My clients, who make it possible for me to be here.

My mom, for initiating me into cooking, and for being my biggest critic.

To Brian, the glue that keeps it all together, and for making me prove to myself that I can do it over and over again.

My staff, who are the threads that weave this wonderful fabric of my work every day and work hard to create the environment that I need to be creative in.

To Rakesh and Rekha Jhunjhunwalla, and Jerry, for believing and supporting me in all my endeavours.

To Hemajee, Esha Deol, Jacqueline Fernandes, Neha Dhupia, Katrina Kaif, Kabir Bedi, Parveen Dusanj, Shekhar Kapur, Vikram Bhatt, Dalip Tahil, and all my other clients for being supportive of my work.

To my family—my brother Vishal, sister Shabana, sister-in-law Puja, Azan, Zara, Uncle Shiv, Aunt Santosh, Uncle Triloknath Sabherwal, Shibs, Gautam, Nikki, Vilaas, and

Bimal. Thank you for the constant encouragement and love.

To Dude—for your unconditional love and companionship for the last thirteen years of my life.

To Lynn and Ajay, who have stood by me through my toughest time as a student of macrobiotics.

To Neelam Rai—for loving me like a mother and caring for me in a way that enriches my life and uplifts me.

To my friends—Upma and the Choraria's, Dilshad, Puja, Sunil, Nisha, Radha, Sarang, Anu, Rahul, Kamal, Shyarmila, Mini, Aunty Sue, Prahlad and Mitali Kakar. Thanks for being with me all these years and making my life happen. I love you guys.

To Dr Raveendara, Dr Keshavan, Dr Narayanan, Krishnakumarjee, and all the staff at Arya Vaidya Chikitsalayam, thank you for making the journey of macrobiotics even more rewarding than it is.

To the Kushi Insitutute staff—Paula, Olaf, Mirea, Mathew; my teachers Bettina, Lucci, John, Warren, Carry, Clyde; my friends from the KI—Mary Nell, Vera Caban, Julie Ong, Connie Arnold; and all the other Level 4 students I was with, my deepest gratitude for being my guides and making me feel like I would get someplace someday.

Finally, to my father—my greatest teacher, friend, and for what he made of me.

A NOTE ON THE AUTHOR

Shonali is India's only practising Counsellor/Chef and Instructor in Macrobiotics and that is her USP. She is a celebrity counsellor and chef to some of the hottest and fittest Bollywood beauties. Her clients include Hema Malini, Neha Dhupia, Esha Deol, Ahana Deol, Jacqueline Fernandez, Katrina Kaif, Tabu, Shekhar Kapur, Kabir Bedi, and Dalip Tahil.

She is a graduate of the Kushi Institute, USA. Her tryst with macrobiotics began in 1998 when her father was diagnosed with cancer, and she wanted to help him with an alternative approach to recovery. She sought a diet that would enhance one's 'well being' from within, focussing on changing blood condition and using food as a tool to change any kind of imbalances in the body and mind. She has been featured in *The Times of India*, *Vogue*, *Elle*, *Hindustan Times*, *DNA,* and so on.

She meets her clients needs not only on the health counselling level, but goes beyond that, wherein she equips you with recipes, cooking classes, and helps you to source products. She is soon to launch her own line of retail products of ready-to-eat snacks and treats under her brand name 'Soulfood'. All of these products are vegetarian, organic, and free from dairy, gluten, yeast, sugar, white processed flour, and non GMOs.

She lives in Mumbai. This is her first book.